Emre Ozsoz, Erick W. Rengifo
Understanding Dollarization

Emre Ozsoz, Erick W. Rengifo

Understanding Dollarization

Causes and Impact of Partial Dollarization on Developing and Emerging Markets

DE GRUYTER
OLDENBOURG

ISBN 978-3-11-044218-2
e-ISBN (PDF) 978-3-11-043702-7
e-ISBN (EPUB) 978-3-11-043403-3

Library of Congress Cataloging-in-Publication Data
A CIP catalog record for this book has been applied for at the Library of Congress.

Bibliographic information published by the Deutsche Nationalbibliothek
The Deutsche Nationalbibliothek lists this publication in the Deutsche Nationalbibliografie; detailed bibliographic data are available on the Internet at http://dnb.dnb.de.

Cover image: TeerawatWinyarat/iStock/Thinkstock
Typesetting: Integra Software Services Pvt. Ltd.
Printing and binding: CPI books GmbH, Leck
♾ Printed on acid-free paper
Printed in Germany

www.degruyter.com

To my wife Ada
To my daughter Elizabeth and my son Francisco
To my grandmother, mother and sisters:
Carmen, Mirtha, Rita y Lucero

To all those people that have always supported me
Erick W. Rengifo

To Banu, Devin and Deniz
Emre Ozsoz

Foreword

The authors of this book, Emre Ozsoz and Erick W. Rengifo, offer a stimulating analysis of dollarization in emerging and developing economies. They discuss major and historical developments regarding partial dollarization and cover the experience of many individual countries in several regions including Latin America, Central and Eastern Europe, Asia and Sub-Saharan Africa. They provide an analysis of motives for dollarization and also discuss pros and cons of dollarization. In addition, they cover the literature on the impact of dollarization on banking systems and financial development and evaluate recent policy interventions in dollarized economies.

It is well known that dollarization is directly related to many major macroeconomic and finance issues as well as key institutional developments in emerging and developing economies. Hence, the book is an excellent reference for scholars specializing in these economies. The book's captivating analysis and findings also offer practical implications for policymakers, financial participants and other key stakeholders.

The book is an excellent reference for students as well. It covers many critical issues on dollarization in an intuitive way and offers useful case studies and individual country experiences. Critical issues and empirical analysis are well articulated. The book can be adopted in upper-level undergraduate courses or master's courses in economics and finance. Those teaching MBA courses may find the book quite useful due to its case study and individual country experience coverage. The book may also be adopted for international business courses.

Whether you are a university student, research fellow, professor or policymaker this book provides interesting and useful information about dollarization in many emerging and developing economies. Any person interested in these economies should have this book on his or her desk.

The authors of "*Understanding Dollarization*" have done an excellent job and can be confident that their enthusiastic work will have many appreciative readers and motivate scholars to engage in further research. The book is timely and will have a significant impact on the field.

Ali M. Kutan
Department of Economics and Finance
Southern Illinois University Edwardsville

Editor, *Emerging Markets Finance and Trade*
Co-Editor, *Economic Systems*
Editor, *Borsa Istanbul Review*

Contents

1 A Primer on Dollarization

1.1 Introduction

Traditionally, each country and economic territory has issued and circulated its own currency. By its most common definition, a currency is a form of fiat money issued by a government and used within a certain economic region. Money can be described by its functions as a medium of exchange (to buy and sell goods and services), as a unit of account (to keep track of revenues, costs and profits), and as a store of value (to save, and smooth consumption over time).

However, it is important to note that in an increasingly globalized marketplace, where not only goods and services but also people and capital move across borders, governments have lost their monopoly over the currency used among their citizens. This is particularly true for emerging economies.[1]

Currency substitution, or *Dollarization*, refers to the use of another country's currency in exchange of or in addition to the local currency. This phenomenon has become widespread in today's global economy.

This definition can be expanded to include the degree by which "real and financial transactions are actually performed in dollars relative to those performed in local currency" (Ortiz, 1983).

The term "dollarization" was coined after the US Dollar, since it has traditionally been the most preferred replacement currency of choice. Nowadays, the term "dollarization" generically refers to the use of another country's currency (not necessarily the US Dollar) in addition to or in exchange of a local currency.

According to FED's estimates as of 2011, almost $538 billion of US currency in print was held outside the US, and nearly two-thirds of all $100 bills were in use outside US borders (Judson, 2012). Considering that 6.7 billion people live outside the US, this translates into an average of 80.3 US dollars in every non-American's pocket worldwide.

Another way of examining the use of foreign currency is to observe the currencies used for international trade transactions (trade dollarization). Table 1.1 shows the percentage use of foreign currencies in global trade finance, and provides an illustration of the relative importance of these currencies on an international scale.

In what follows in this chapter, we explain the concept of dollarization in detail and consider several important aspects of dollarization. The remainder of the chapter proceeds as follows. Section 1.2 defines different types of dollarization. Section 1.3

1 Emerging markets are economies that display some of the hallmarks and efficiencies of a developed economy, but still lack development in some sectors. These economies include countries such as Argentina, Chile, Colombia, Hungary, India, Peru, Turkey, Mexico, Hong Kong, Indonesia and Brazil, among others.

Table 1.1: Percentage participation of several currencies in trade finance.

Currency	**%**
EUR	42.09
USD	31.12
GBP	8.48
JPY	2.41
AUD	2.18
CAD	1.89
CHF	1.83
SGD	1.04
SEK	0.98
HKD	0.96
NOK	0.87
THB	0.76
RUB	0.61
CNY	0.51
DKK	0.51

Data as of September 2012.
Source: SWIFT.

provides an overview of the causes of dollarization, and Section 1.4 discusses the peculiarities of banking in a dollarized economy. Section 1.5 provides a brief historic description of dollarization around the globe, and Section 1.6 discusses the impact of different exchange rate regimes and their relationship with dollarization.

1.2 Asset vs Currency Substitution

Before we proceed with a more detailed analysis of dollarization and its causes, it is important to distinguish between two causes that determine the demand for foreign currencies and assets: currency and asset substitution.

Asset substitution is centered on portfolio allocations where investments in foreign currency denominated assets are determined based on their positive and larger expected returns and their marginal contribution to the risk of the overall portfolio.[2] This phenomenon is particularly notable in high inflation environments, where local economic agents look for ways of obtaining positive real interest rates.[3] In order to achieve real returns, local investors typically select assets that are denominated in

2 We recommend the reader to refer to the Capital Asset Pricing Model (CAPM) to understand this relationship.

3 Real interest rates are the nominal interest rates adjusted for inflation. More detail is provided in Chapter 3. The basic principle is that agents seek a return that allows them to protect their purchasing power.

hard currencies—for example, the US dollar or Euro—that provide a greater degree of protection against inflation and isolate their portfolios from local currency risk.

On the other hand, *currency substitution* refers to the use of foreign currency to *replace* the roles of local currency with regard to its use as a unit of exchange and as a unit of account. We explain some of the reasons behind this in the following chapters.

1.3 Official and Partial Dollarization

The dollarization phenomenon is observable in different forms. Some countries may choose to give up their local currency entirely and adopt another country's currency as legal tender. This type of dollarization is known as **"official"** or **"de jure"** dollarization and is observable in more than ten countries (Table 1.2).

Countries decide to embark on a path of full dollarization for a number of valid reasons. Amongst these motives are the desire to eliminate sudden and strong currency depreciations, to reduce the interest rates on their (public and private) international loans by reducing depreciation risk premiums, to attract more foreign direct investment and portfolio investment and to cut the costs of servicing debt. Dollarization can be judged as a commitment towards low inflation, fiscal discipline and transparency (Berg and Borensztein, 2000).

Heavily dollarized economies carefully consider depreciation risk. Economies with high ratios of dollarized loans (public and private) and large capital inflows are particularly vulnerable to sudden depreciation pressures. As we describe in more detail later, a sudden and large depreciation of local currency automatically raises

Table 1.2: A selection of countries and territories that are officially dollarized.

Countries that have adopted the US dollar as legal tender	Countries that have adopted the euro as legal tender	Countries using a third currency as legal tender
British Virgin Islands	Andorra	Cook Islands (New Zealand Dollar)
Caribbean Netherlands	Kosovo	Nauru (Australian Dollar)
East Timor[a]	Mónaco	Lesotho (South African Rand)
Ecuador[a]	Montenegro	Macau (Hong Kong Dollar)
El Salvador	San Marino	Palestinian Territories (Israeli Shekel)
Marshall Islands	Vatican City	Turkish republic of Northern Cyprus (Turkish lira)
Micronesia		
Palau		
Panama[a]		
Turks and Caicos		

[a] Uses its own coins.
Source: Edwards and Magendzo (2003).

the value (in local terms) of the outstanding balance on a dollar-denominated loan, which negatively affects not only public finances, but also the finances of citizens and firms who have foreign currency denominated loan obligations. Consequently, such currency depreciation can cause banking crises and social unrest as citizens see their wealth eroded.

However, even though currency risk is reduced by full dollarization, it is possible that the interest rates charged on public debt will not decrease due to the existence of other risk factors. For instance, a country's default or sovereign risk (measured as the spread between yields on local currency bonds over US Treasuries) may implicitly reflect other fundamental information about the health of the economy. This information could include the existence of political instability, a lack of national security, growing income inequality, poverty and social unrest or other such socio-economic variables. Such risks may not be properly assessed by analyzing currency risk alone.

Another perceived benefit of full dollarization is that it allows greater integration of the country's financial system with the financial markets of developed economies, thus providing a platform for sustainable economic growth in international trade as importers and exporters are able to access currency and settle trades with greater efficiency.

The benefits of full dollarization are not free. The most obvious cost is that fully dollarized countries lose their monetary and exchange rate policy tools. These policies are relevant in certain extreme circumstances; for instance, when the international price of a certain export commodity that is integral to maintaining the country's fiscal stability falls dramatically. We demonstrate the costs of the loss of control over monetary policy control through a simplified example that looks at the evolution of prices for a ton of iron ore.

Assume that the total cost per ton equals US$ 45.[4] Now assume that we have two countries, one fully dollarized (country A) and another non or partially dollarized (country B). Let us assume the exchange rate in country B, in January 2011, was 2.5 local currency units per US$. This implies that in that month, the production cost was equal to 112.5 local currencies per ton. Finally, assume that the production cost is set in local currency, that it is constant in time and that the components of the costs (basically labor) are kept at January 2011 values.

4 As an example, we can use the production cost of a corporation (African Minerals) that used to have operations in a developing country (Sierra Leone). For African Minerals, its average production cost during 2013 was equal to US$ 44.5 per ton (page 32 of its 2013 annual report). This production cost is more than double the number reported by competitors (Rio Tinto and BHP Billiton) that consider US$ 20 or less as their production cost. For example, Rio Tinto mentioned that "The company's production cost in 2014 averaged US$ 19.50 per ton. By factoring in the current exchange rate for the Australian dollar, and lower oil and gas prices, Rio's iron ore costs are now running closer to $US17." (http://www.theguardian.com/business/2015/apr/17/rio-tinto-well-thrive-on-lower-iron-ore-prices-while-others-suffer-says-boss).

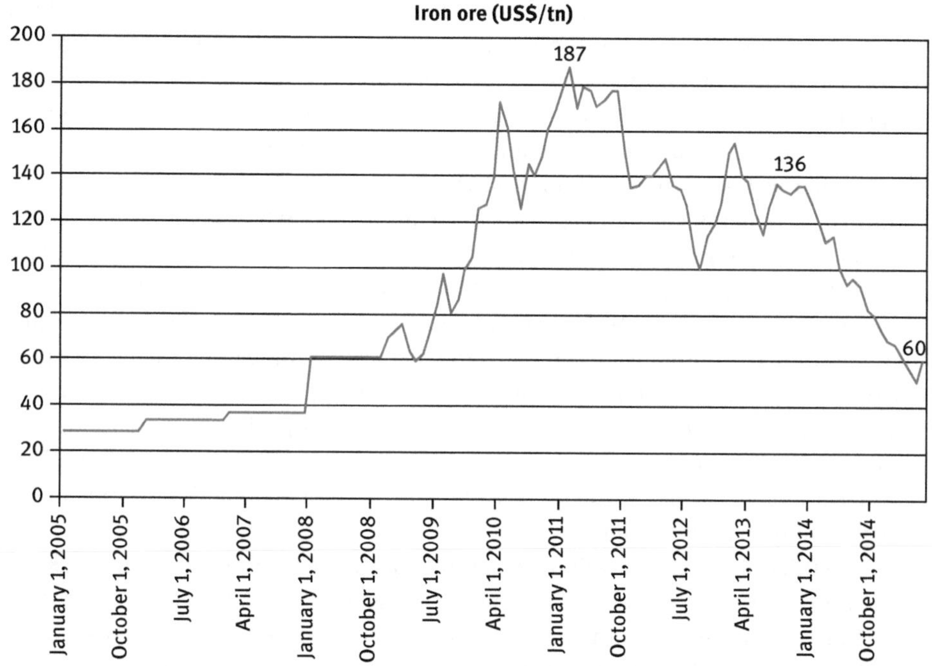

Figure 1.1: Iron ore price evolution.

As observed in Figure 1.1, in January 2011 the international price of iron ore was at US$ 187 per ton and dramatically fell to US$ 60 by the beginning of 2015. In this circumstance, the ratio of local production cost to international price rises in country A from 24% (45/187) to 75% (45/60). What happens in country B clearly depends on its exchange rate. Let us assume two scenarios, one in which the exchange rate in January 2015 is the same as the one in 2011 (2.5 local currency per USD) and a second scenario where the local currency depreciates to 3.5 per US$.

If the exchange rate of country B remains the same, the ratios of production costs to the international price are the same as those observed in country A: 25% ((45 × 2.5) / (187 × 2.5)) and 75% ((45 × 2.5) / (60 × 2.5)). However, in the second scenario, country B is in a better position: 25% ((45 × 2.5) / (187 × 2.5)) in January 2011 and 54% ((45 × 2.5) / (60 × 3.5)) in January 2015.[5,6]

5 The numerator is multiplied by 2.5 (the January 2011 exchange rate) because we have assumed that the prices of the components of the costs are valued in local currencies and that they do not change during this period. This is something that is observed in reality in the short term. The denominator is multiplied by 3.5 (the January 2015 exchange rate) since this is the actual price in local currency received per ton of iron ore.

6 It is also important to see the other side of the coin. If local currencies depreciate, this implies that imports are more expensive and, if the pass through is high, the negative effect of the depreciation can overcome the benefits received.

Many researchers and politicians alike argue that a government's ability to adjust the exchange rate to manage the negative effects of adverse price movements is important to maintain socio-economic stability, and that the loss of these tools by fully dollarizing an economy can have serious negative repercussions that reverberate throughout the economy and even stunt future growth prospects.

Another well-known cost of full dollarization is the loss of seigniorage for these countries. In general, seigniorage refers to a country's ability to issue local currency (non-interest paying debt). However, seigniorage is also referred to all the monies the central banks keep from private institutions, for which they do not pay any type of interest (private banks' reserve requirements, for example). It is for these reasons that seigniorage is normally measured by the increases in base money (currency plus reserves). Seigniorage is complemented by the profits governments make when they issue non-interest paying debt (currency) and buy interest-paying assets (such as government securities, loans to private banks, etc.). This power is lost when full dollarization is adopted. As the central bank's ability to use monetary policy disappears, so does its ability to issue currency.

Once full dollarization is adopted, central banks effectively need to buy back the stock of domestic currency held by depository institutions. If central banks do not have enough reserves to do this, they would be required to borrow reserves, which would consequently increase transition costs.

Finally, an additional problem with full dollarization is the loss of the central banks' capacity to act as the lenders of last resort in situations of extreme need (e.g. in the circumstance of systemic bank runs). The ability of central banks to act as lenders of last resort depends on their ability to issue more currency in order to ensure that all deposits in local currency will be fully protected.[7] In a fully dollarized economy, the central bank's response is limited by the level of international reserves it has at the moment of the crisis, and by its ability to obtain dollar-denominated loans from international sources while suffering from liquidity problems.

As we have seen in Table 1.2, fully dollarized economies are not common. For most economies, dollarization is a **de facto** process during which local currency slowly loses its roles as a medium of exchange, a unit of account and a store of value in favor of other "hard" currencies. During this process, big ticket items such as cars or houses start being denominated in foreign currency; banks begin to offer saving accounts in foreign currency or offer accounts that are indexed to a foreign currency. This type of dollarization is known as **"de facto"** or **"partial"** dollarization, and this de facto dollarization is main type of dollarization analyzed in this book.

---

7 More than ever, countries are implementing systems to insure deposits using market mechanisms that allow for risk sharing, in an attempt to cover potential systemic and non-systemic risks that banks can face. One example of this organization/risk insurance mechanism is the Federal Deposit Insurance Corporation (FDIC) in the USA.

1.4 Measuring the Degree of Partial Dollarization

Research on dollarization (especially partial dollarization) is often hindered by the lack of availability of precise data. One main reason for this paucity of data is that there is no feasible way of accounting for foreign currency circulating in an economy, especially outside the banking system—foreign currency banknotes in the hands of agents in an economy cannot be accurately counted until they are deposited into the banking system. However, not all foreign currency in an economy makes its way to depository institutions.

In partially dollarized economies, economic agents might hold a significant amount of their savings "under the mattresses" for various reasons (i.e. tax avoidance, lack of trust in the banking system, or the fear of being questioned on the origins of their income, particularly if this income was gained through fraudulent means). This makes dollarization measurement a challenge, forcing us to rely on proxies that provide estimates on the level of dollarization in a particular economy.

The most commonly used measures for dollarization in a partially dollarized economy are based on the amount of foreign currency deposits, total liabilities or loans in the banking system.

The ratio of these variables to total deposits (also referred to as deposit dollarization) or to total liabilities (liability dollarization) or to the amount of loans (loan dollarization) in the banking system is used as the measure of the level of dollarization as a whole in an economy. While these ratios do not provide us with an exhaustive picture of the degree of currency substitution in an economy, they are still important proxy measurements that allow researchers to study dollarization from an objective standpoint.

Tables 1.3–1.5 provide dollarization data on different measures of dollarization, compiled from various sources.

1.5 Causes of Dollarization

In this section, we first describe the most likely causes of official (full) dollarization, and then present the causes of partial dollarization.

Edwards and Magendzo (2003) divide officially dollarized countries into two groups based on the reasons that led them to fully dollarize. The first group includes *independent nations* that have chosen to use a third country's currency as legal tender; these countries include Ecuador, El Salvador, Andorra, Micronesia, Vatican City and Monaco. The second group encompasses *territories* or *colonies* within a national entity, for instance, Puerto Rico, US Virgin Islands, Guam, Greenland and American Samoa.

For small independent nations, official dollarization is adopted due to these countries' proximity to and political and economic ties with a hard-currency partner.

Table 1.3: Liability dollarization—foreign currency liabilities to total liabilities ratio.

	Foreign-currency-denominated liabilities to total liabilities, ratio (%)									
	2005	**2006**	**2007**	**2008**	**2009**	**2010**	**2011**	**2012**	**2013**	**2014**
Argentina	16.6	16.7	17.1	18.8	20.2	19.3	15.6	10.0	10.4	9.9
Austria		20.0	17.2	19.4	14.4	11.3	12.0	10.6	10.0	9.9
Bosnia and Herzegovina						67.0	66.2	65.2	65.1	
Brazil	13.5	11.8	13.4	16.5	10.4	10.7	13.1	13.6	14.3	14.9
Bulgaria				60.0	64.4	58.6	54.8	51.8	50.2	49.0
Burundi						21.5	19.9			
Canada	37.6	37.9	36.2	44.1	38.3	36.3	40.6	42.4	42.7	49.2
China, P.R.: Hong Kong							61.1	59.7	62.5	62.5
Denmark	24.7	25.7	29.4	29.0	26.5	26.4	25.7	22.7	23.4	22.0
Finland						28.2	28.8	28.7	30.3	
France				26.2	24.3	13.4	12.3	11.1	12.2	
Germany	10.1	10.4	10.1	10.2	9.0	8.7	8.5	8.5	8.5	9.4
India							7.1	6.9	8.2	10.7
Indonesia	19.9	17.1	18.3	20.0	17.8	16.5	16.3	18.6	24.4	22.9
Italy	12.4	15.3		22.5	45.7	33.9	30.7	27.8	28.7	32.0
Korea, Republic of				14.9	12.7	13.4	14.9	14.4	14.3	
Latvia				80.7	89.9	87.9				
Luxembourg				29.1	28.8	32.8	31.8	33.8	35.3	36.5
Mexico	11.4	6.5	7.8	12.2	11.3	10.4	13.5	12.2	12.3	15.6
Netherlands				22.5	19.7	21.8	22.4	19.7	20.6	21.3
Peru										
Poland				20.5	19.9	21.1	23.2	21.2	20.2	
Portugal	7.4	8.1	8.2	5.8						
Romania			45.9	43.7	42.8					
Russian Federation				33.3	31.5	28.2	26.1	25.1	25.4	34.7
Seychelles				58.8	43.5					58.6
Slovak Republic				21.7	2.8	3.2	4.1	3.6	3.9	4.2
South Africa				5.1	4.3	4.1	4.5	5.7	6.3	8.1
Spain	24.5	23.0	23.7	24.4	24.2	24.2	24.0	24.5	24.7	27.3
Sri Lanka							12.0	11.3		
Switzerland				62.5	56.1	54.7	53.2	49.9	47.0	49.3
Turkey	41.4	43.1	38.7	40.0	36.7	35.5	41.6	41.2	47.5	48.3
Uganda						29.2	32.9	36.2	38.1	39.2
United Kingdom				73.8	66.8	67.4	69.3	15.8	16.1	
Uruguay				78.4	70.5	69.5	67.9	67.0	68.6	

Source: IMF—Financial Soundness Indicators.

Table 1.4: Loan dollarization—foreign currency loans to total loans.

Foreign-currency-denominated loans to total loans, ratio (%)						
	2009	**2010**	**2011**	**2012**	**2013**	**2014**
Argentina	12.7	13.6	12.8	6.6	4.5	4.5
Austria	22.4	22.1	21.4	19.7	18.8	18.8
Bosnia and Herzegovina		70.0	66.9	63.1	63.2	
Brazil	12.7	11.7	13.0	13.8	15.2	15.9
Bulgaria	58.7	61.3	63.7	64.0	61.2	57.0
Burundi		0.7	0.6			
Canada	25.9	27.4	28.2	26.8	27.7	30.1
China, P.R.: Hong Kong			37.8	40.2	44.2	45.0
Denmark	25.4	25.7	23.4	21.3	21.2	18.2
Finland		24.0	23.3	16.8	20.3	
France	2.3	11.0	14.0	10.8	11.5	
Germany	11.5	11.5	11.0	10.5	10.0	11.5
India			7.3	7.4	8.4	12.2
Indonesia	14.9	15.6	16.6	15.2	17.0	16.3
Italy	9.9	9.2	8.9	8.3	8.8	9.5
Korea, Republic of	12.6	13.8	15.0	13.2	12.8	
Latvia	92.1	92.7				
Luxembourg	27.9	29.7	29.0	30.7	33.5	35.9
Mexico	9.7	9.6	11.4	25.7	26.8	30.7
Netherlands	17.0	19.7	18.0	17.5	19.2	22.7
Poland	32.2	32.5	34.4	30.5	28.5	
Romania	59.9					
Russian Federation	29.9	27.0	25.4	21.3	22.7	29.4
Seychelles	37.2					25.6
Singapore	41.9	43.6	47.0	45.1	45.7	49.4
Slovak Republic	2.0	1.5	1.6	1.5	1.1	1.9
South Africa	7.0	6.7	9.1	8.3	8.7	10.0
Spain	22.1	25.5	26.7	27.9	27.9	27.2
Sri Lanka			17.3	17.8		
Switzerland	47.9	46.7	47.0	45.1	43.0	45.0
Turkey	24.9	25.8	27.9	25.0	27.1	27.8
Uganda		27.1	29.1	40.7	41.2	43.7
United Kingdom	53.9	52.6	58.0	52.9	55.4	
Uruguay	66.1	61.2	61.9	61.8	58.0	
Vietnam	16.5	11.4	9.5	8.0		

Source: IMF—Financial Soundness Indicators.

Table 1.5: Deposit dollarization—foreign currency deposits to M2 money supply.

	Foreign currency deposits as a ratio of M2 money supply (%)																
	1990	1991	1992	1993	1994	1995	1996	1997	1998	1999	2000	2001	2002	2003	2004	2005	2006
Albania	NA	NA	NA	NA	18.80	18.69	21.94	18.30	16.81	18.17	19.39	22.63	22.53	22.30	23.01	26.45	29.49
Angola						7.30	29.40	42.90	53.00	66.90	67.60	NA	NA	NA	NA	NA	NA
Argentina	33.70	35.01	35.37	40.65	43.88	44.83	46.56	46.54	49.16	52.27	55.68	64.39	0.92	1.72	2.90	NA	NA
Armenia	NA	NA	19.37	46.72	39.78	19.68	21.37	34.27	40.62	48.53	49.26	46.82	36.61	42.92	62.97	NA	NA
Belarus	NA	NA	NA	NA	NA	NA	NA	NA	NA	NA	57.91	55.52	44.00	40.32	36.66	27.97	22.43
Bolivia	58.29	62.61	65.71	68.66	59.42	63.45	68.86	68.41	68.98	70.11	70.25	58.68	56.64	56.29	55.32	NA	NA
Bulgaria	NA	33.62	24.77	19.91	31.75	25.66	45.32	38.34	35.94	34.97	32.67	37.09	32.93	32.76	34.94	NA	NA
Cambodia	NA	NA	NA	36.22	51.39	56.33	63.08	62.57	54.22	60.95	68.22	69.71	69.15	69.34	61.29	NA	NA
Costa Rica	31.95	39.84	32.44	30.26	30.00	37.12	33.47	34.75	38.16	35.67	36.33	39.63	40.19	40.26	46.74	44.28	40.71
Croatia	NA	NA	NA	54.06	50.25	57.45	59.57	61.70	66.29	65.75	64.62	67.79	62.09	59.06	58.08	55.75	48.08
Czech Rep.	NA	NA	NA	8.13	6.99	5.30	6.03	11.35	11.40	11.72	11.60	11.12	9.98	9.05	8.93	NA	NA
Egypt	NA	50.73	37.26	26.68	23.68	25.41	23.18	19.64	18.16	17.28	18.78	21.32	23.18	27.34	28.44	24.54	24.43
Estonia	NA	NA	NA	NA	10.88	10.39	10.31	15.28	15.70	14.48	19.31	17.21	16.64	15.85	15.45	20.35	20.27
Georgia	NA	NA	NA	NA	80.10	30.80	14.80	20.80	29.10	35.40	NA	NA	NA	NA	NA	NA	NA
Hungary	NA	NA	NA	NA	NA	NA	NA	NA	NA	NA	NA	NA	NA	20.82	26.25	31.61	28.85
Jamaica	NA	NA	NA	NA	NA	NA	NA	NA	19.10	19.16	25.60	23.42	27.92	35.84	36.57	36.47	NA
Lithuania	NA	NA	NA	44.20	26.90	26.80	24.80	21.30	24.20	30.40	34.00	NA	NA	NA	NA	NA	NA
Macedonia	NA	NA	NA	NA	NA	19.96	18.82	23.54	26.07	34.90	28.46	64.14	40.52	42.63	45.27	NA	NA
Malaysia	NA	NA	NA	NA	NA	NA	5.76	11.81	15.51	17.99	23.62	24.82	20.09	23.09	25.71	NA	NA
Mexico	NA	3.77	3.90	3.39	5.84	6.80	6.35	3.96	4.36	4.79	6.49	7.12	6.66	NA	NA	NA	NA
Moldova	NA	NA	NA	17.97	11.44	12.34	10.98	10.53	29.32	38.32	39.58	38.17	44.13	51.36	44.03	42.26	56.65
Mongolia	NA	NA	7.50	33.00	19.50	20.50	24.20	29.00	23.80	24.70	NA	NA	NA	NA	NA	NA	NA
Morocco	NA	NA	NA	NA	NA	NA	42.96	54.60	47.04	54.45	15.92	23.80	15.89	24.10	NA	NA	NA
Nicaragua	NA	NA	NA	NA	NA	58.70	55.39	56.94	56.98	59.61	61.20	69.61	70.42	67.43	62.42	NA	NA
Nigeria	NA	NA	NA	NA	7.33	25.34	16.78	14.03	19.92	53.83	38.72	35.98	65.11	52.54	59.45	NA	NA

Table 1.5: (continued)

	Foreign currency deposits as a ratio of M2 money supply (%)																
	1990	1991	1992	1993	1994	1995	1996	1997	1998	1999	2000	2001	2002	2003	2004	2005	2006
Pakistan	2.56	8.77	11.70	13.62	12.78	12.20	15.24	20.94	22.55	9.18	7.62	9.34	NA	5.57	5.33	NA	NA
Peru	29.68	47.73	52.33	58.58	57.39	56.39	60.92	53.45	52.72	53.32	54.51	52.46	57.44	55.43	53.53	NA	NA
Philippines	17.31	17.82	20.85	22.36	20.26	20.92	26.11	28.84	29.32	27.38	28.46	27.41	26.59	27.63	28.48	NA	NA
Poland	NA	NA	NA	NA	NA	NA	NA	NA	14.93	14.70	14.10	14.86	14.15	13.46	12.08	12.54	NA
Romania	2.25	2.53	11.98	21.46	17.67	17.44	18.00	22.05	24.53	29.30	30.87	42.19	37.19	39.26	37.28	NA	NA
Russia	NA	NA	NA	29.50	28.80	20.00	19.40	17.60	30.40	29.50	26.90	NA	NA	NA	NA	NA	NA
Singapore	NA	NA	NA	3.30	7.78	16.26	15.83	10.82	16.38	12.60	13.97	15.82	14.67	15.62	16.96	NA	NA
Slovak Rep.	NA	NA	NA	11.22	12.90	11.31	10.17	10.51	14.65	14.48	15.63	15.54	15.23	11.97	12.80	NA	NA
Slovenia	NA	NA	NA	NA	42.67	44.67	45.34	38.01	33.17	33.52	36.90	36.82	34.77	34.16	36.23	35.92	NA
Turkey	23.26	30.41	34.80	39.45	48.87	50.14	48.55	51.32	47.25	45.01	44.02	56.04	53.96	45.08	NA	33.07	NA
Ukraine	NA	NA	7.93	20.56	31.75	22.76	16.68	13.33	20.78	24.35	22.74	18.33	18.76	20.69	24.07	23.58	NA
Venezuela	NA	NA	NA	NA	0.87	NA	NA	NA	0.08	3.24	1.68	2.55	NA	NA	NA	NA	NA
Vietnam	NA	NA	26.15	20.93	NA	19.93	19.60	22.12	25.29	28.13	29.72	31.17	28.66	23.12	23.22	22.40	19.79

Source: Kutan, Ozsoz, and Rengifo (2012).

In the case of Andorra, Monaco or San Marino, it made perfect sense to adopt the Euro as legal tender. The relatively small size of these economies and each country's economic and political ties with surrounding EU states made using the Euro a necessity.[8]

There are other economies that are larger than the aforementioned group, yet also adopted a foreign currency for reasons other than economic or political ties. For instance, Ecuador and El Salvador have chosen this option to control their runaway inflationary problems. This appears to be one common factor in almost all episodes of dollarization, official and partial; dollarization follows periods of high and persistent inflation. Central and South American countries are fertile ground for the examination of this phenomenon. A number of Central and South American economies—for example, Peru and Nicaragua—experienced bouts of high inflation in the 80s and early 90s, and to this day, the government and citizens of these countries remain acutely aware of the difficulties of daily life in a period of high inflation. Consequently, it is no coincidence that nowadays, Latin American economies are some of the most heavily dollarized economies in the world. To illustrate, as of 2013, almost 70% of all liabilities in the Uruguayan banking system are denominated in foreign currency.

In the case of Ecuador, the inflation rate fell from an annual rate of 96% to an average of 6% following the adoption of the US Dollar in 2000, as can be observed in Figure 1.2.[9]

The same relationship is observable in other partially dollarized economies. Turkey experienced chronic high inflation throughout the 80s and 90s. The average inflation rate in the 80s was 51%, and during the 90s, average inflation climbed to over 75%, hitting 106% in 1994 (Source: IMF-IFS). As a corollary, the dollarization of bank accounts also reached its peak level in that year. The average ratio of foreign currency deposits in the banking system to overall bank deposits rose to 50% in 1994 (see Figure 1.3).

Countries transitioning from a centrally controlled economy to a market economy, such as Russia and Bulgaria, experienced similar bouts of high inflation. Both economies experienced hyperinflationary periods in the 90s, with inflation reaching 1,058% in Bulgaria in 1997 and 874% in Russia in 1993. Both countries also witnessed

8 Andorra has never had a currency of its own. Prior to adoption of the Euro by its two neighbors (France and Spain), the country was using the French Franc and the Spanish Peseta as its legal currency. When France and Spain adopted the Euro in 2002, Andorra also adopted the Euro. Monaco used the French Franc prior to the adoption of the Euro, and issued its own French Franc coins with the permission of the French government. Following the switch to the Euro, Monaco was allowed to issue its Euro coins but the country cannot issue Euro banknotes ("The Euro outside the Euro area")

9 Hidalgo (2010) mentions that the inflation rate fell from an annual rate of 37.5% to an average of 6.8% following the adoption of the US Dollar in 2000. The numbers presented above come from the author's own research.

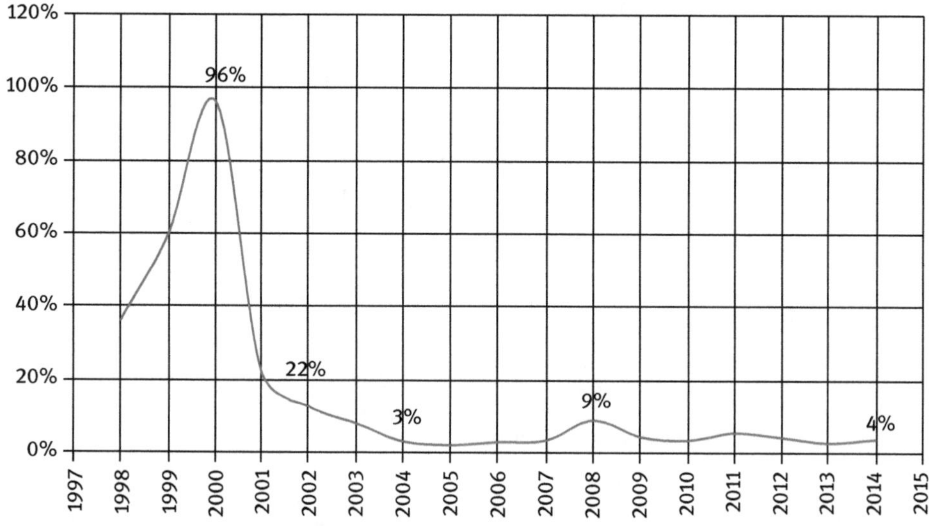

Figure 1.2: Inflation dynamics in Ecuador.
Source: (Until 2005) Index Mundi (http://www.indexmundi.com/g/g.aspx?c=ec&v=71). (From 2006) Ecuador en Números (http://www.ecuadorencifras.gob.ec/indice-de-precios-al-comunidor-2013/).

their dollarization rates reach their peaks in these years. For Russia, the dollarization ratio (measured as a percentage of foreign currency account balances in the banking system to overall bank deposits) was over 40% in 1993; in Bulgaria, this same ratio climbed to over 53% in 1993.

The link between inflation and dollarization can be understood by realizing that in countries with high inflationary processes, foreign currency provides a shelter from domestic inflation and enables agents to retain the value of their financial assets. In this regard, dollarization emerged not only as a natural hedge, but also as an incentive to save in high inflation economies. Some studies have shown that by providing this incentive, dollarization also helped stem capital flight from those economies (Feige, 2003). Figure 1.4 shows this relationship for the case of Peru.

1.6 Dollarization and Banking Dollarization

As mentioned previously, a major problem that academics and industry professionals face when working on the dollarization phenomenon is the limited availability of data, compounded by the issue of inadequate datasets that do not fully capture the true extent of countries' dollarization. As we have already mentioned, one common metric used to measure dollarization is the ratio of foreign currency deposits in the banking system to the size of overall deposits. Another commonly used metric is the

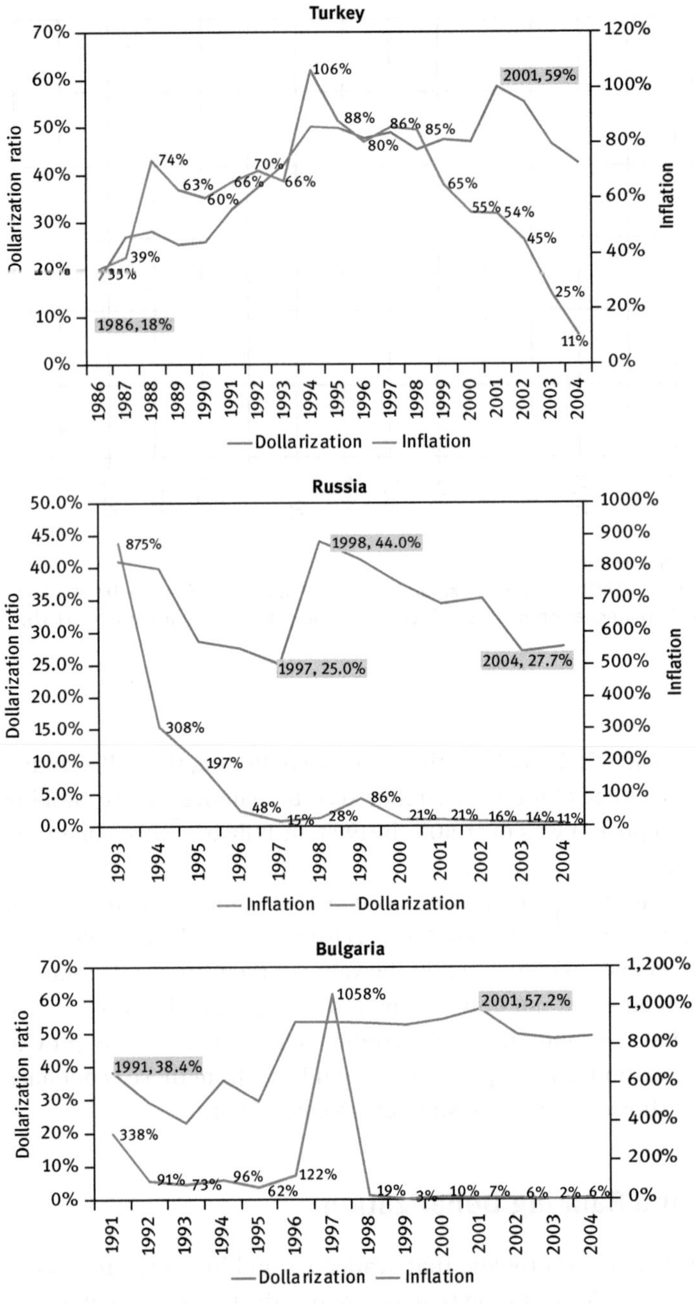

Figure 1.3: Dollarization and inflation in selected economies.
The figures show dollarization ratios and inflation rates in selected dollarized economies. Dollarization is measured as the ratio of foreign currency deposits in the banking system to total bank deposits.
Source: IMIF-IFS, Yeyati (2006).

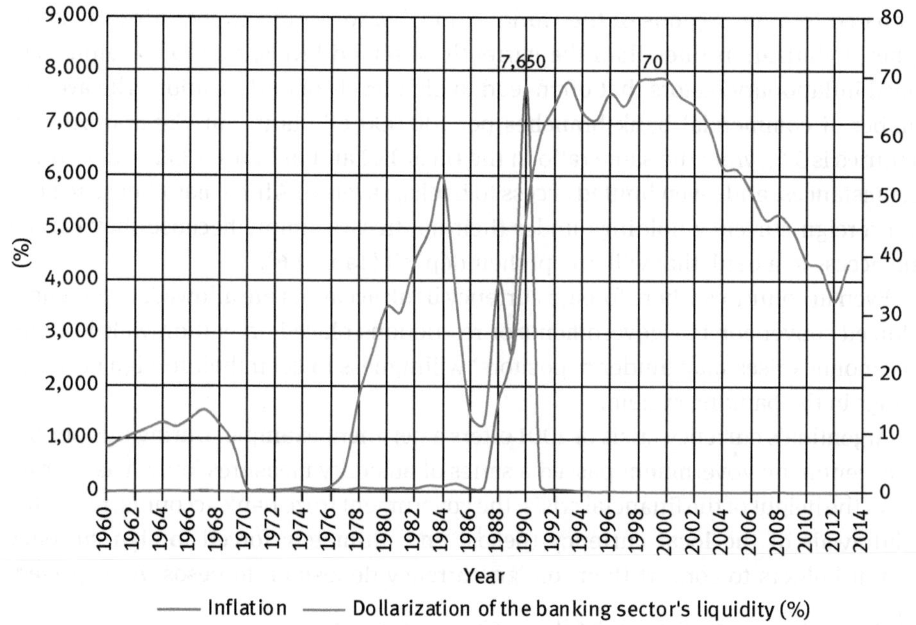

Figure 1.4: Dollarization and inflation in Peru (1959–2013).
Source: Central Reserve Bank of Peru (https://estadisticas.bcrp.gob.pe/estadisticas/series/anuales).

ratio of foreign currency deposits in the banking system with respect to a measure of the money supply, either the M1 or the M2.[10] Note that in high inflation environments where the M2 figure might be unnaturally inflated, it may be more appropriate to employ the M1 measure of the money supply rather than M2.

When data regarding actual foreign currency holdings is unavailable, using these metrics to approximate the extent of the dollarization of an economy is necessary, but sometimes yields inaccurate results. The quality of the approximation depends on many factors, including the ability to open bank accounts in foreign currencies (financial services availability).

Countries where opening a foreign currency account is allowed show high dollarization ratios compared to countries where such accounts are not permitted or are not available.[11] This partly explains why Africa, which has low banking penetration and generally low quality financial institutions, shows lower dollarization ratios

10 M1 is part of the money supply that includes all coins and currency in circulation as well as demand deposits, checking accounts and negotiable order of withdrawal (NOW) accounts. M2 is a broader classification of money supply that includes M1 and savings and small time deposits, overnight repos and non-institutional money market accounts.

11 Note that there are other reason why individuals can choose not to save their money in their banking systems: weak rule of law; low quality of institutions; lack of property rights; lack of deposit insurance; possibility of forced conversions and retentions (incapacity of retiring funds), among others.

compared to other regions of the world. Normally, we would expect Africa to show higher dollarization rates than the currently observed levels, due to the aforementioned inflationary factors that often lead to high levels of dollarization. The average number of commercial bank branches per 100,000 adults in Sub-Saharan African countries is 5.6, while the same ratio in the US is 35.3 and in Europe 33.2. Under these circumstances, and given limited access to banks, savers in Africa may choose to keep their foreign currency holdings under their mattresses simply because they cannot gain access to a bank that will accept their deposit (Table 1.6).

Even in countries where foreign currency bank accounts are allowed, experiences of forced conversions by governments or restrictions placed on withdrawals in times of economic crises may hinder depositors' willingness to keep their foreign currency savings in the banking system.

Argentina's currency crisis of 2001 offers a pertinent example. During this period, the Argentinean government passed a series of austerity measures known as "*corralito;*" at the height of the financial crisis, the government froze bank accounts, restricted withdrawals of the local currency (pesos) and ultimately forced foreign currency account holders to convert their foreign currency deposits into pesos. As expected,

Table 1.6: Banking penetration in sub-Saharan African economies.

Sub-Saharan Africa		**Commercial bank branches (per 100,000 adults)**	
Sub-Saharan Africa (Average)		**5.6**	
Angola [AGO]	11.4	Liberia [LBR]	3.6
Benin [BEN]	3.5	Madagascar [MDG]	1.7
Botswana [BWA]	8.6	Malawi [MWI]	3.3
Burundi [BDI]	2.5	Mali [MLI]	3.9
Cabo Verde [CPV]	30.6	Mauritania [MRT]	4.9
Cameroon [CMR]	1.7	Mauritius [MUS]	21.6
Central African Republic [CAF]	0.9	Mozambique [MOZ]	3.8
Chad [TCD]	0.6	Namibia [NAM]	7.2
Comoros [COM]	1.4	Nigeria [NGA]	5.8
Congo, Dem. Rep. [ZAR]	0.7	Rwanda [RWA]	7.6
Congo, Rep. [COG]	2.9	Sao Tome and Principe [STP]	23.7
Cote d'Ivoire [CIV]	4.6	Seychelles [SYC]	48.3
Equatorial Guinea [GNQ]	5.5	Sierra Leone [SLE]	3.0
Ethiopia [ETH]	2.9	South Africa [ZAF]	10.4
Gabon [GAB]	7.5	South Sudan [SSD]	0.9
Gambia, The [GMB]	8.8	Sudan [SDN]	2.9
Ghana [GHA]	5.7	Swaziland [SWZ]	7.1
Guinea-Bissau [GNB]	2.5	Tanzania [TZA]	2.2
Kenya [KEN]	5.5	Uganda [UGA]	2.6
Lesotho [LSO]	3.4	Zambia [ZMB]	4.4

Table 1.6 shows the number of commercial bank branches per 100,000 people in selected sub-Saharan countries.
Source: World Bank.

the amount of foreign currency held within the banking system in Argentina fell dramatically following the crisis (Figure 1.5).

Thus, it is important to note that deposit dollarization in several countries banking systems can hide the real magnitude of dollarization. In aggregate, people understand their political environment and the strength (or lack thereof) of their institutions, and accordingly decide where keep their dollar deposits (and deposits in general) based on their faith in the banking system or government.

Another way to see the existence of ***hidden*** dollarization is to observe the constant growth and use of "black" or "shadow" markets. A black or shadow market is an unofficial market where individuals and even corporations change their foreign currency holdings in order to obtain local currencies (sell dollars) or to obtain foreign currency (buy dollars).

Black markets are common mechanisms for investors in particular and individuals in general to exchange foreign currency in countries where government restrictions prohibit such transactions. The percentage difference between the official exchange rate and the prevailing rate in the black market is usually referred to as the **black market premium**. During times of uncertainty and restricted foreign currency supply through official channels (such as central bank auctions), the premium usually rises. For instance, following the escalation of tension between Ukraine and Russia in the winter of 2015, the black market exchange rate for the US dollar in Ukraine reached 21.5 Hryvnia while the official exchange rate was 16.2 Hryvnia.

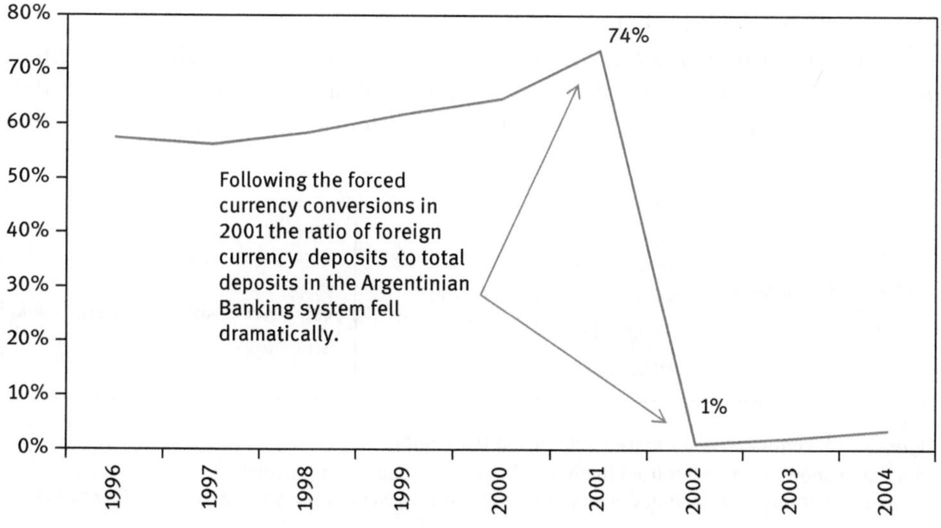

Figure 1.5: Ratio of foreign currency deposits to total deposits in Argentina.
Figure 1.5 shows the ratio of foreign currency deposits in the Argentinian Banking system to total deposits.
Source: Yeyati (2006).

In Argentina, capital controls instituted by the government have made it difficult and costly for agents to buy and sell foreign currencies. The government has issued restrictions on the percentage of individuals' salaries that can be converted into USD. Moreover, as a way to reduce the use of USD, dollar purchases are taxed up to 20%.[12] This government attempt to prevent capital flight has been largely unsuccessful, as its citizens continue to dump Pesos to look for more stable currencies to protect their savings and to realize their everyday transactions. Argentinean citizens have developed a well-organized and dynamic black market for the purchase and sale of foreign currencies, especially US dollars. These unofficial markets are informally arranged and organized in certain streets in Buenos Aires (as well as in several other cities in Argentina). One can observe several buyers/sellers openly advertising their exchange services. Moreover, almost all Argentinean newspapers publish daily black market exchange rates, known as "Dólar blue" or "Mercado Paralelo". Figure 1.6 is a screenshot from the website of La Nación, the largest and one of the most respected newspapers in Argentina. As we can see, this newspaper lists both the official and the unofficial (or Dólar blue) exchange rates.[13]

In Figure 1.6 one can also observe the spread between buy and sell prices and also the spread between official and parallel market exchange rates. The buy / sell spread is 9.690 and 9.720 in the official market and 14.660 and 14.730 in the black market.

Another example of the black market premium can be seen in Nigeria, where the government has pegged its exchange rate to the US Dollar. As of November 2015, the difference between the official and black market exchange rates was close to 20 Naira, or in other terms, 10% of the official spot rate of 198 Naira per dollar (Source: bra research, Nigeria) (Figure 1.7).

Following the above discussion, it is obvious that in dollarized economies where foreign currency accounts are permitted (common practice in most dollarized economies), banks face particular challenges. In such economies, the

Cotización
Dólar oficial

DÓLAR COMPRA	DÓLAR VENTA
$ 9, 690	$ 9, 720

Dólar Ahorro (Retiro antes de 1 año)	$ 11, 664
Dólar Tarjeta / Turista	$ 13, 122
Dólar Soja	$ 6, 318
Dólar Bolsa	$ 14, 590

Cotización
Dólar blue o dólar paralelo

DÓLAR BLUE COMPRA	DÓLAR BLUE VENTA
$ 14, 660	$ 14, 730

Figure 1.6: Argentinean black market ("Mercado Paralelo").
This figure shows a snapshot from the Argentinean newspaper "La Nación".
Source: "Dólar Hoy," La Nación, December 5, 2015, http://www.lanacion.com.ar/dolar-hoy-t1369.

12 Gould, "Argentina's Control Strategies," https://www.thefinancialist.com/argentinas-control-strategies-2/.

13 "Dólar Hoy," *La Nacion*, December 5, 2015, http://www.lanacion.com.ar/dolar-hoy-t1369.

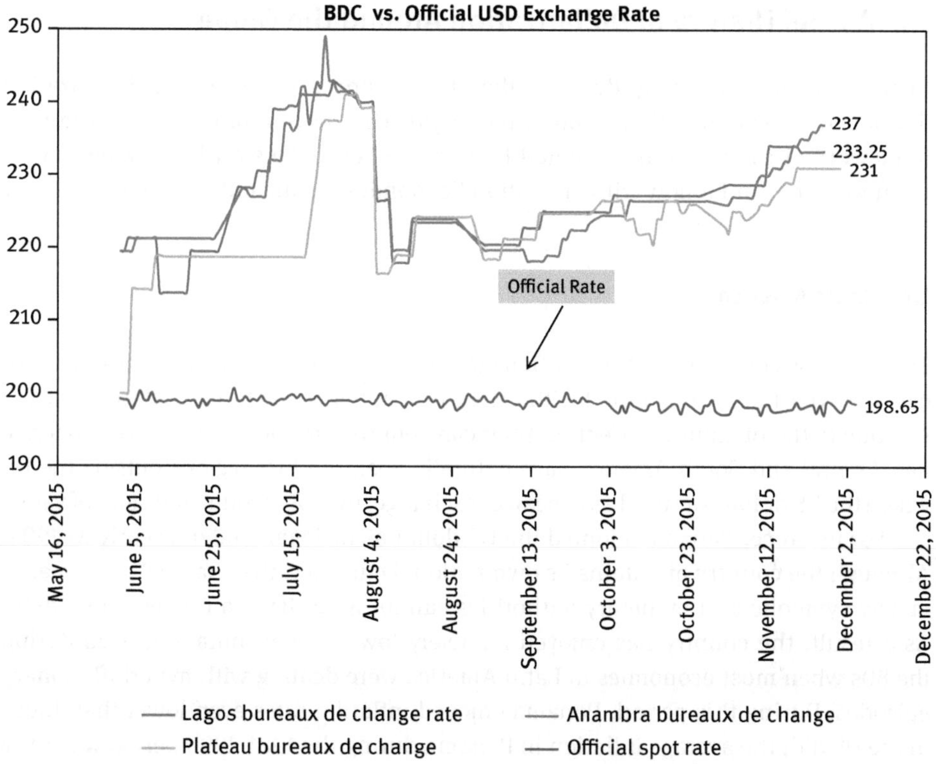

Figure 1.7: Nigerian Naira official spot rate vs black market exchange rate ("Bureaux de Change Rate").
Figure 1.7 shows the official Naira-USD rate vs the black market exchange rate (Bureaux de Change Rate) in three Nigerian states (Lagos, Anambra and Plateau).
Source: bra Research, Lagos, Nigeria.

problem of a mismatch in banks' assets and liabilities arises. Even though banks may hedge against this risk by using derivative instruments such as foreign currency swaps, in most dollarized economies, the financial system may not be sophisticated enough for such hedging options to be available. As a result, banks may simply counter their foreign currency liabilities by creating foreign currency denominated assets such as foreign currency denominated loans. However, this practice does not necessarily remove banks' foreign currency risk but transforms it into another form of risk known as "default risk". Studies (such as Kutan, Ozsoz and Rengifo, 2012) have shown that because of this transformation, the dollarization of the banking system has a pervasive effect on bank profitability and system stability. We will investigate this dimension of dollarization in more detail in upcoming chapters.

1.7 A Brief History of Dollarization Around the Globe

In this section, we briefly describe the circumstances under which dollarization developed in several regions around the world. This section provides the historical framework of the material presented later in the book. We start by looking toward Latin America, and follow with Transition Economies, Asian and African economies.

1.7.1 Latin America

The first cases of currency substitution started in Latin America, where local currencies were (partially) substituted with the US dollar, hence the term "dollarization".

Due to the proximity of Central American countries to the US and close economic ties, Central and South America have naturally been the first regions outside the US where the US dollar was used as a mean of exchange, unit of account and store of value.

For instance, Panama adopted the US dollar as its legal tender as early as 1904. Although the country maintains its own national currency, the "Balboa", its usage is mostly symbolic and monetary authorities cannot issue Balboa-denominated debt. As a result, the country has enjoyed relatively low levels of inflation, even during the 80s when most economies in Latin America were dealing with hyperinflationary episodes. During this period, Panama enjoyed inflation rates even lower than those in the US did; the average inflation in Panama during the 1981–1990 period was 1.8% while the same rate in the US was 4.7% (Calvo and Veigh, 1992) (Figure 1.8).

However, Panama was an exception in Latin America. Most countries continued using their own currencies as legal tender, while their citizens turned to US Dollars as their primary currency of choice for their savings. For instance, as of 1935, almost 35% of all demand deposits in the Mexican banking system were in US dollar denomination (Ortiz, 1983). Table 1.7 provides the dollarization ratios of selected Latin American economies and their average inflation rates.

Among the dollarized Latin American economies, two stand out from the crowd: *Bolivia and Uruguay*. Starting in the 80s, these countries have seen dollarization ratios rise to and exceed 50%. As of 2003 (Levy-Yeyati, 2006), the ratio of foreign currency deposits to the overall deposits in the Bolivian banking system was close to 93%. For Uruguay, the same ratio reached as high as 88% for the same year, declining to 69% by 2013 (IMF-FSI.)

In the case of Bolivia, the shift toward dollarization has long historical roots, tracing back to the 1960s when the country started to rely on foreign currency loans from international banks to finance its development programs (Morales, 2003). These loans required payments in the same currency, locking Bolivia in a foreign currency loan trap and further increasing its reliance on foreign currency financing.

The hyperinflationary episodes experienced during the 80s were also another instigating factor in the country's dollarization story. Inflation in Bolivia reached

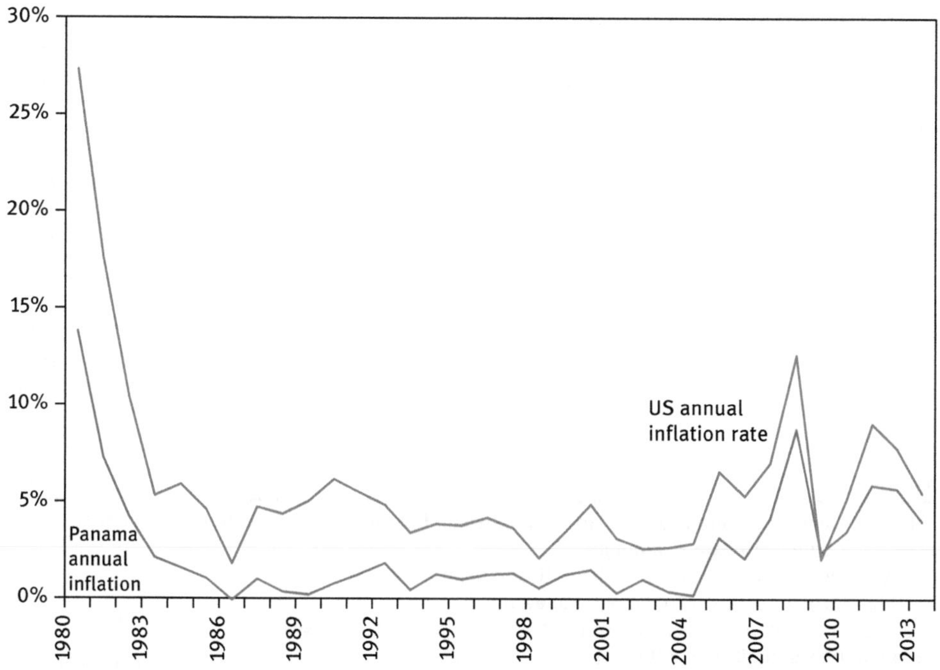

Figure 1.8: Inflation rates in Panama and in the US (1980–2013).
Figure 1.8 shows the annual inflation rates in the US and in Panama between 1980 and 2013.
Source: World Bank.

11,750% in 1985 (See Figure 1.9). The average inflation rate between 1982 and 1986 was 2,741%. The Central bank in Bolivia conducted monetary policy in local and foreign currency using "the standard instruments and the standard IMF type of monetary programming" (Morales, 2003). However, this policy was not successful. In the second half of the 90s, dollarization ratios increased even further, reaching their peaks in 2003. The effects of the East Asian Financial Crisis and the devaluation of Latin American currencies were major factors in the rise of dollarization ratios at this time.

In the case of Uruguay, inflationary episodes were not as severe as in the case of Bolivia. Uruguay's highest inflation rate between 1980 and 2000 was experienced in 1992, when inflation reached 112%. However, inflation was still a persistent phenomenon in Uruguay during the 80s, as illustrated in Figure 1.10. Inflation rates did not fall below 18% (1982) and during the 90s, inflation remained consistently high (with the average around 48%). Inflation rates eventually fell to single digits at the end of the 90s, reaching 5.7% in 1999 (IMF, IFS).

In the case of Peru, the ratio of foreign currency deposits in the banking system remained consistently above 70% until 2001, after which it started a steady decline. The monetary authorities were able to control inflation by 1995. However, even though inflation considerably decreased to single digit levels after 1996, foreign currency

Table 1.7: Dollarization ratios for selected Latin American economies.

Country	Average dollarization (%)	Average inflation (%)	Period
Argentina	15.5[a]	9.45	2005–2014
Bolivia	63.5[b]	7.94	1990–2004
Chile	20.2[c]	3.15	2004–2014
Colombia	0[a]	20.97	1990–2000
Costa Rica	47.4[b]	12.73	1987–2014
Dominican Republic	9[a]	6.54	1996–2000
Ecuador	24[a]	39.03	1990–1999[d]
El Salvador	45[a]	13.98	1980–2000[e]
Honduras	29.6[a]	7.09	2001–2014
Paraguay	42[a]	26.89	1988–2000
Peru	55.3[b]	9.9	1992–2014
Uruguay	76[a]	33.88	1981–2013
Venezuela	1.89[b]	22.02	1998–2001

Table 1.7 shows the average dollarization ratios and inflation rates for selected Latin American economies subject to data availability.
[a] Foreign currency liabilities to total liabilities in the banking system.
[b] Foreign currency deposits to the M2 money supply.
[c] Ratio of foreign currency deposits to total deposits in the banking system.
[d] Ecuador fully dollarized in 2000.
[e] El Salvador fully dollarized in 2001.
Source: IMF-IFS, Bank of Chile, Central Reserve Bank of Peru, Banco Central de Costa Rica, IMF-FSI, Yeyati (2006).

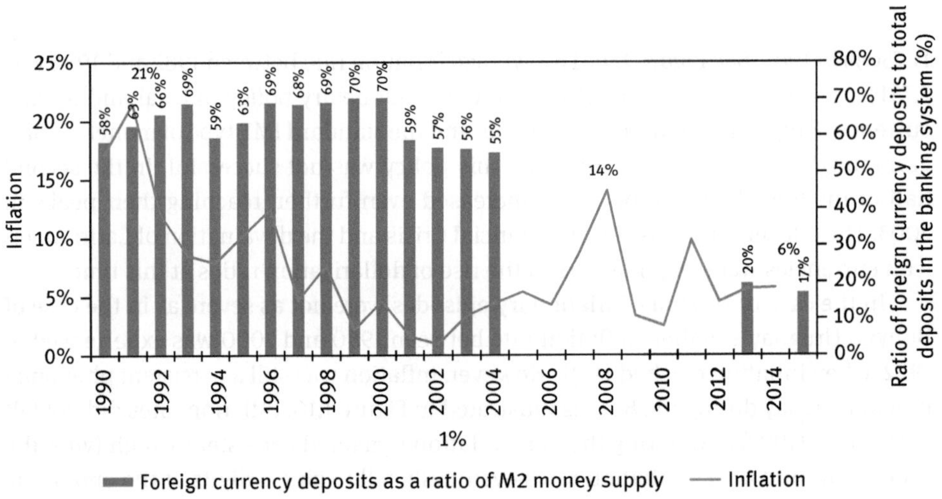

Figure 1.9: Dollarization ratios and inflation rates in Bolivia (1990–2014).
Figure 1.9 shows the inflation rate in Bolivia between 1980 and 2014.
Source: IMF-IFS and IMF-FSI.

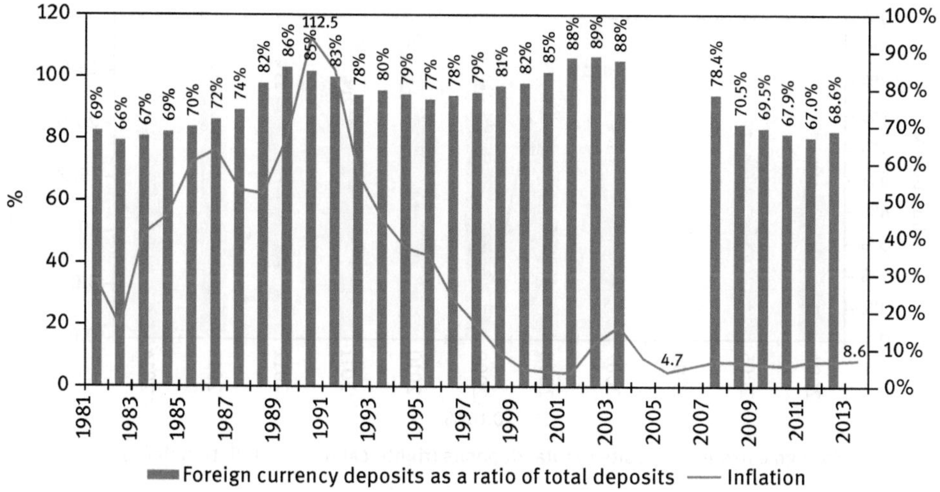

Figure 1.10: Inflation rates and dollarization in Uruguay (1981–2013).
The figure shows the inflation rate in Uruguay between 1981 and 2013. Dollarization measure used is the ratio of foreign currency deposits in the banking system to total deposits.
Source: IMF-IFS, IMF-FSI and Yeyati (2006).

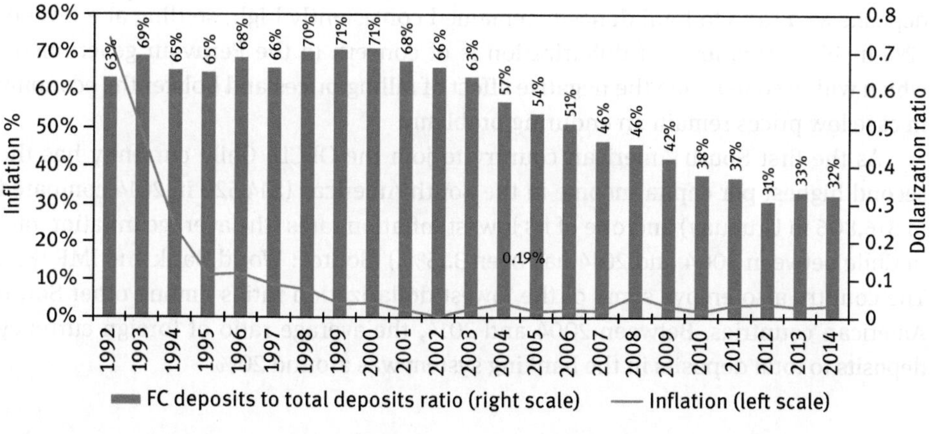

Figure 1.11: Inflation rates and dollarization in Peru (1992–2014).
Figure 1.11 shows the inflation rate and dollarization ratios in Peru between 1992 and 2014. The dollarization measure used is the ratio of foreign currency deposits in the banking system to total deposits.
Source: IMF-IFS, Banco Central De Reserva Del Perú.

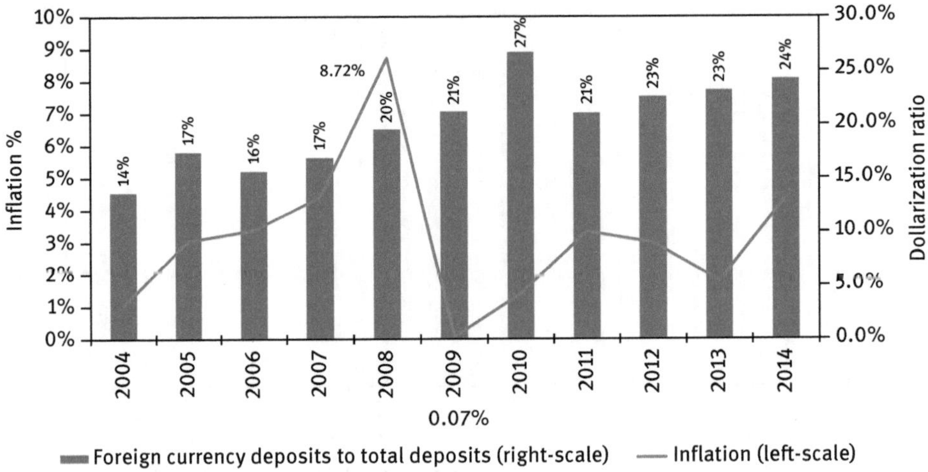

Figure 1.12: Inflation rates and dollarization in Chile (2004–2014).
Figure 1.12 shows the inflation rate and dollarization ratios in Chile between 2004 and 2014. The dollarization measure used is the ratio of foreign currency deposits in the banking system to total deposits.
Source: IMF-IFS, Banco Central de Chile.

deposits as a ratio to total deposits remained consistently high, settling at a level of 32% in 2014. This level of dollarization is of concern to the Peruvian government, which will need to tackle the negative effect of falling prices and bolster the economy in case low prices remain an enduring problem.

As the first South American country to join the OECD, Chile currently has the second highest per capita income in the South Americas ($14,528 in 2014 compared to $16,806 in Uruguay) and one of its lowest inflation rates (the average inflation rate in Chile between 2004 and 2014 has been 3.15%.) (Source: World Bank and IMF-IFS). The country also enjoys some of the lowest dollarization ratios among other South American countries. Between 2004 and 2014, the average ratio of foreign currency deposits to total deposits in the banking system was around 20%.

1.7.2 Transition Economies

The dollarization episodes seen in Latin America in the 70s and 80s were repeated in Transition[14] Economies during the 90s. The fall of the Berlin Wall and the end of the

14 Transition economies are defined as economies that are transitioning from a centrally planned economy to a market economy. These countries include the former Soviet Bloc economies in Central and Eastern Europe and in Central Asia.

communist regimes in Eastern Europe and in former Soviet Bloc economies marked the start of increasingly high rates of dollarization in these countries.

The runaway inflation experienced in these economies was a major cause of the currency substitution processes, much as it was in the case of Latin America during the 80s. As shown in Table 1.8, high dollarization ratios are correlated with high levels of inflation. For instance, among the fifteen countries presented in the table, Croatia has experienced the highest levels of dollarization. As illustrated in Figure 1.13, between 1994 and 2014, the dollarization ratio in the Croatian economy remained persistently high. The average ratio of foreign currency deposits in the banking system to total deposits for this period was 60.9%. It is also no coincidence that this country has experienced one of the highest inflation rates in Europe in recent years. The annual inflation rate in Croatia in 1993 was 1494%. Mainly due to the civil turmoil experienced in former Yugoslav countries at the time, the inflation rate fell to 107.15 in 1994 and sharply dropped to 4.45 in 1995. Although the inflation rate has stayed in single digits from 1995 until today, dollarization rates have not decreased in this country. On the other hand, the Czech Republic, which has had the lowest dollarization ratios in the group (around 9%), also had one of the lowest inflation levels in the sample (less

Table 1.8: Dollarization ratios for selected transition economies.

Country	Average dollarization (%)	Average inflation (%)	Period
Albania	27[a]	8.90	1994–2008
Belarus	43[b]	54.86	2000–2005
Bosnia and Herzegovina	66[a]	103.87	2010–2013
Bulgaria	55[a]	3.45	2008–2014
Croatia	60.9[b]	8.12	1994–2014
Czech Rep.	9[b]	5.98	1994–2003
Estonia	15[b]	11.37	1994–2006
Latvia	29[b]	10.02	1994–2004
Lithuania	26[b]	13.98	1994–2004
Macedonia	34[b]	3.56	1995–2004
Moldova	44[b]	18.22	1999–2004
Poland	13[b]	6.21	1998–2003
Romania	28[b]	46.06	1995–2004
Slovak Rep.	13[b]	8.09	1998–2003
Slovenia	37[b]	8.59	1994–2005
Ukraine	21[b]	13.06	1999–2005

Table 1.8 shows the average and median dollarization ratios and inflation numbers in selected transition economies during the 1990s and early 2000s.
[a] Foreign currency deposits to total deposits in the banking system.
[b] Foreign currency deposits to the M2 money supply.
Source: Bank of Albania, National Bank of republic of Belarus, Bulgarian National Bank, Croatian National Bank, Czech National Bank, Bank of Estonia, Bank of Latvia, Bank of Lithuania, Nat. Bank of the Rep. of Macedonia, National Bank of Moldova, National Bank of Poland, National Bank of Romania, National Bank of Slovakia, Bank of Slovenia, National Bank of Ukraine.

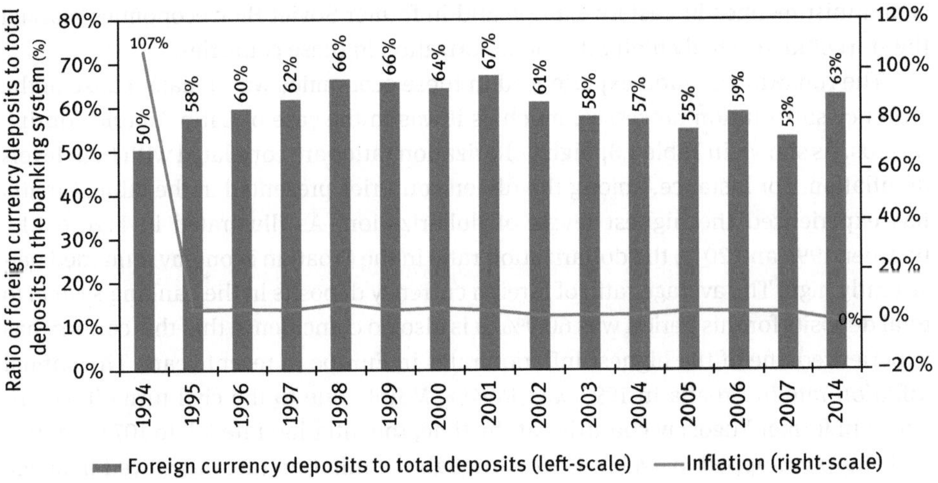

Figure 1.13: Dollarization and inflation in Croatia.

than 6%) and did not experience an inflationary period like Croatia did during its transition process to a market economy.

Figure 1.14 shows the evolution of dollarization and inflation in Albania between 1994 and 2008. Despite a drop in the inflation rate from a record high of 33% in 1997, the dollarization ratio in the country kept rising throughout the 2000s. The persistently high ratio of dollarization can be partially attributed to the large flow of remittances from Albania's neighboring countries, reaching a level as high as 15% of the

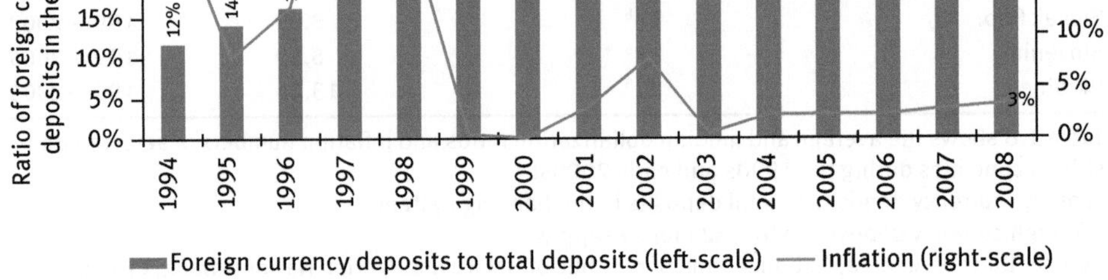

Figure 1.14: Dollarization and inflation in Albania.
Source: National Bank of Albania, IMF-IFS.

country's GDP at the beginning of the 2000s. Remittances make up a large portion of savings in the Albanian economy and are usually deposited in the original currency (Manjani, 2015). This illustrates that although inflation has been a major source of dollarization in Albania (at least during the last years of the 90s), it was nevertheless not the only determinant of dollarization, as can be the case for other regions and countries around the world.

1.7.3 Asia

Among Asian economies, observed dollarization ratios were not uniform. Developed Asian economies such as Singapore show relatively low rates of deposit dollarization (the ratio of foreign currency deposits to the M2 money supply in Singapore averaged 15% between 2000 and 2004) while exhibiting high liability dollarization figures—an average of 45% between 2009 and 2014.

Some of the less-developed Asian economies such as Cambodia have the highest dollarization rates on the continent. The average ratio of foreign currency deposits to the M2 money supply in Cambodia is 67% between 2000 and 2004 (see Table 1.9).

1.7.4 Sub-Saharan Africa

As indicated earlier, measured dollarization rates are relatively lower in Africa; one of the reasons for this situation is the low banking penetration rates in Africa and the use of banking system statistics for dollarization measurements. Table 1.10 shows some available statistics.

1.8 Exchange Rate Regimes and Dollarization

The exchange rate regime followed by a country's monetary authorities has a crucial impact on the country's dollarization experience. In fact, official dollarization is usually referred to as an extreme example of a fixed exchange rate regime.

In a fixed exchange rate system, the monetary authorities usually peg the value of the local currency to an anchor currency or to a basket of currencies and stand ready to intervene in the forex markets to defend their peg. The dollar and the Euro are usually the most widely used anchor currencies.[15] The monetary authority that is authorized to maintain the fixed exchange rate system in a country is also called *a currency board*. Separate from the monetary authority of the country, a currency board cannot determine monetary policy and does not lend to the country's government. Currency

15 Recently the Chinese Yuan has been gaining prominence as an anchor currency.

Table 1.9: Dollarization ratios in selected Asian economies.

	2000 (%)	2001 (%)	2002 (%)	2003 (%)	2004 (%)	2005 (%)	2006 (%)	2007 (%)	2008 (%)	2009 (%)	2010 (%)	2011	2012	2013	2014
Cambodia[a]	68.22	69.71	69.15	69.34	61.29										
China, P.R.: Hong Kong[b]												37.80%	40.20%	44.15%	45.02%
India[b]												7.27%	7.42%	8.39%	12.17%
Indonesia[b]										14.94	15.64	16.57%	15.20%	17.00%	16.34%
Korea, Republic of[b]										12.59	13.79	15.00%	13.22%	12.85%	
Malaysia[a]	23.62	24.82	20.09	23.09	25.71										
Pakistan[a]	7.62	9.34		5.57	5.33										
Phillippines[a]	28.46	27.41	26.59	27.63	28.48										
Singapore[b]										41.88	43.65	46.99%	45.10%	45.74%	49.40%
Singapore[a]	13.97	15.82	14.67	15.62	16.96										
Sri Lanka[b]												17.33%	17.78%		
Vietnam[b]										16.49	11.41	9.53%	8.01%		
Vietnam[a]	29.72	31.17	28.66	23.12	23.22	22.40	19.79								

[a] Foreign currency deposits as a ratio of M2 money supply (Source: Kutan, Ozsoz and Rengifo, 2012)
[b] Foreign currency denominated loans to total loans ratio (Source: IMF—financial soundness indicators (FSI)).

Table 1.10: Dollarization ratios in sub-Saharan Africa.

	2000 (%)	2001 (%)	2002 (%)	2003 (%)	2004 (%)	2005 (%)	2006 (%)	2007 (%)	2008 (%)	2009 (%)	2010 (%)	2011 (%)	2012 (%)	2013 (%)	2014 (%)
Angola[a]	83.70	81.00	85.04	73.64	71.90										
Angola[b]	67.60														
Burundi[c]											21.47	19.87			
Cape Verde[a]	6.24	5.39	4.58	4.43	4.78										
Congo, Dem rep.[a]	43.50	57.00	66.95	84.87	85.96										
Djibouti[a]	58.36	55.83	54.53												
Gambia, The[a]			11.35												
Ghana[a]	30.80	33.16	33.22	30.84	29.31										
Kenya[a]	15.50	15.20	16.04	14.82	18.09										
Liberia[a]			85.28	88.33	89.68										
Malawi[a]	22.00	14.60	20.44	19.17	20.08										
Nigeria[b]	38.72	35.98	65.11	52.54	59.45										
Sierra Leone[a]	22.62	34.25	31.33	30.28	33.49										
South Africa[c]									5.11	4.30	4.13	4.52	5.72	6.25	8.12
Sudan[a]	38.54	40.57	40.46	39.29	39.51										
Uganda[a]	29.90	34.59	31.43	35.17	35.47										
Uganda[c]											29.25	32.86	36.17	38.06	39.15
Zambia[a]	53.20	42.70	44.44	41.05											
Zimbabwe[a]				6.80	12.00										

[a] Foreign currency deposits as a ratio of total deposits in the banking system (Source: IMF—financial soundness indicators [FSI]).
[b] Foreign currency deposits as a ratio of M2 money supply (Source: Kutan, Ozsoz & Rengifo, 2012).
[c] Foreign currency liabilities as a ratio of total liabilities as a ratio of total liabilities (Source: IMF—financial soundness indicators [FSI]).

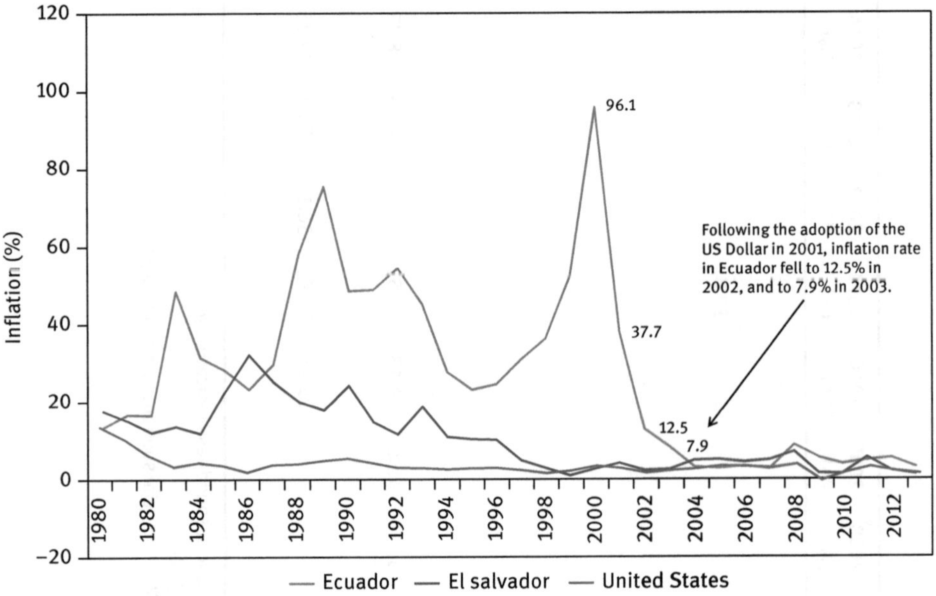

Figure 1.15: Inflation rates in Ecuador, El Salvador and the US.
The figure above shows the annual inflation rates in Ecuador, El Salvador and the US prior to and after the adoption of the US dollar as legal tender. El Salvador adopted the US currency in 2000 and Ecuador in 2001.
Source: World Bank.

boards usually have no restrictions on current and capital account transactions; they buy and sell foreign currency in an attempt to maintain the pegged exchange rate to the US dollar. Examples of currency boards include the Hong Kong Monetary Authority–which also acts as the country's de facto central bank–and the Bermuda Monetary Authority, which issues the country's national currency and maintains its peg to the US dollar.

In the case of a free float or a flexible exchange rate system, market forces determine the value of the local currency. The monetary authorities do not provide an explicit or implicit guarantee as to the value of the local currency vis-à-vis other currencies.

There are several variations within each system. A *free-float* is a flexible exchange rate regime where the monetary authorities adopt an observatory approach to the forex markets while in the case of a *dirty-float* regime, the monetary authorities may intervene in currency markets to control the value of the local currency or the inflation rate.

Variations among fixed exchange rate regimes are also common. The best example is official dollarization. Official or full dollarization can be considered as an extreme case of fixed exchange rate regime where the monetary authority adopts the anchor currency as the legal tender. This can also be regarded as an example of a currency union with the adopted country's economy, but on a unilateral basis. The monetary authority of the adopted currency usually does not provide any guarantees (such as providing loans in the event of liquidity problems) to the adopting nation's monetary authorities, thus the country that fully dollarizes gives up its monetary power in exchange for stability in financial and real markets.

In general, over time, the interest rates and the inflation rate in the adopting country converge to those in the adopted currency's economy. Ecuador and El Salvador both enjoyed inflation rates similar to the US inflation rate upon their adoption of the US dollar as legal tender in 2000 and 2001 respectively. In the case of El Salvador, the inflation rate converged to that of the US almost immediately, while in the case of Ecuador, it took three years for the inflation rate to converge fully to that of the US (see Figure 1.15).

2 Pros and Cons of Dollarization

2.1 Introduction

As defined in the previous chapter, dollarization refers to the use of a foreign money by economic agents (households, corporations and governments), for activities (unit of exchange, savings or unit of account) normally carried out in a local currency. Dollarization has its roots in serious economic problems that posed real threats to agents' purchasing power in particular and their wellbeing in general. However, dollarization's impact needs to be adequately understood in a more holistic way that involves analyzing not only the short and medium term effects of changing to a foreign currency, but also the long-term effects of such a change, while considering various socio-economic variables that are crucial ingredients for a sustainable and stable economic development.

In this chapter, we briefly present several benefits and disadvantages of dollarization by evaluating the most common arguments used for and against the adoption of a foreign currency.

In the following section, we list some of the arguments that provide support for dollarization. We carefully evaluate arguments regarding transactions costs and the incentive to save under inflationary processes, among other factors.

Once the benefits are considered, we then look at some of the arguments against dollarization. We present some macro level factors that include the loss of monetary policy control, the inability to use exchange rates as an economic policy instrument and the incapacity to act as a lender last resort or conduct seigniorage. Furthermore, we describe the micro impacts of dollarization, such as its impact on exchange rate volatility and impact upon the appreciation/depreciation of savings and credit.

In part 2, we present the arguments in favor of full and partial dollarization; Section 2.3 provides a discussion of the arguments against these two types of dollarization.

2.2 Arguments in Favor of Dollarization

Dollarization is studied under two generic forms: full and partial. Under full dollarization the country's monetary authority gives up its local currency and adopts the currency of another country such as the US dollar or the Euro. Examples of countries that have chosen a policy of full dollarization include Panama, Ecuador and El Salvador, where the US dollar is used as legal tender, and Montenegro, Andorra and Kosovo, where the Euro is legal tender.

Observing the type of dollarization a country undergoes—full or partial—is important in order to evaluate the benefits and costs of the phenomenon; as we shall see, the costs and benefits of each type of dollarization differ greatly. We divide this section accordingly.

Most of the debate surrounding dollarization has centered on the reasons why countries decide to fully dollarize. In the case of several Latin American countries which have battled with high and chronic inflation for years, adopting the US Dollar has always been a viable option to restore purchasing power. Moreover, these countries often have strong existing economic ties to the US. The US is commonly the biggest trade partner for Latin countries, and is also an important source of remittances, which play a significant role in a number of Latin American economies.

Table 2.1 shows the top trade partners for South and Central American economies and the volume of trade between these countries and their trade partners. We can observe that the US is the leading partner for the two regions. Close to half of all exports from South America and over 60% of those from Central America are bound for the US. The United States is also the major source of imports for these economies. 56% of all imports to Central America and 43% of all imports to South America originate in the US.

As illustrated in Table 2.2, the aggregate remittances to Latin America and the Caribbean were almost $50 billion at the end of 2014, with Mexico accounting for nearly half of this amount.

There are several principal reasons for adopting a policy of dollarization. Firstly, dollarization acts to moderate the impact of inflation in economies that have suffered from high and chronic inflationary conditions. Secondly, dollarization compels governments to act with an increased degree of financial discipline. Thirdly, dollarization reduces the costs of borrowing. Finally, transaction costs relating to foreign trade are reduced under a system of dollarization. In the following section, we describe each of these benefits in detail.

Table 2.1: Top trade partners and trade volume.

	South America		Central America	
	Exports to	**Imports from**	**Exports to**	**Imports from**
In terms of trade volume (in mils of USD as of 2013)				
The United States	$10,541	$9,878	$1,790	$1,106
Germany	$2,352	$1,796	$116	$94
Japan	$1,035	$2,156	$110	$44
Other Countries	$9,134	$9,069	$859	$727
In terms of trade ratio				
The United States	46%	43%	62%	56%
Germany	10%	8%	4%	5%
Japan	4%	9%	4%	2%
Other Countries	40%	40%	30%	37%

Source: OECD.

Table 2.2: Remittances to Latin America and the Caribbean.

Remittances received (in current billions of USD—2014 figures)	
Latin America & Caribbean (Aggregate)	$48.13
Mexico	$24.46
Guatemala	$5.84
El Salvador	$4.24
Colombia	$4.17
Brazil	$2.65
Caribbean small states	$2.35
Bolivia	$1.18
Panama	$0.76
Costa Rica	$0.59
Argentina	$0.50
Chile	$0.14
Uruguay	$0.12
Belize	$0.08
Dominica	$0.02
Dominican Republic[a]	$4.49
Ecuador[a]	$2.46
Grenada[a]	$0.03
Honduras[a]	$3.14
Haiti[a]	$1.78

[a] 2013 figures.
Source: World Bank.

2.2.1 Inflation Reduction

For countries facing high and chronic inflation and economic instability due to high exchange rate volatility (which is then transferred to high price volatility), full dollarization provides a quick fix.

As has been observed when analyzing the experiences of countries that have fully dollarized, the adoption of another country's currency has a positive impact on inflation expectations and brings inflation levels close to those of the adopted currency's home country. As mentioned in Chapter 1, Ecuador's inflation rate fell from 37.5% to an average of 6.8% following the adoption of the US Dollar in 2000 (Hidalgo, 2010). In the case of El Salvador, the average inflation rate in the 21 years (between 1980 and 2001) preceding the adoption of the US Dollar was 14%, reaching its peak in 1986 (32%). Following the adoption of the US Dollar in 2001, the inflation rate dropped to 3.75% and fell further to 1.87% in 2002. The historical inflation rates of Ecuador and El Salvador, which fully dollarized in 2000 and 2001 respectively, are presented in Figure 2.1.

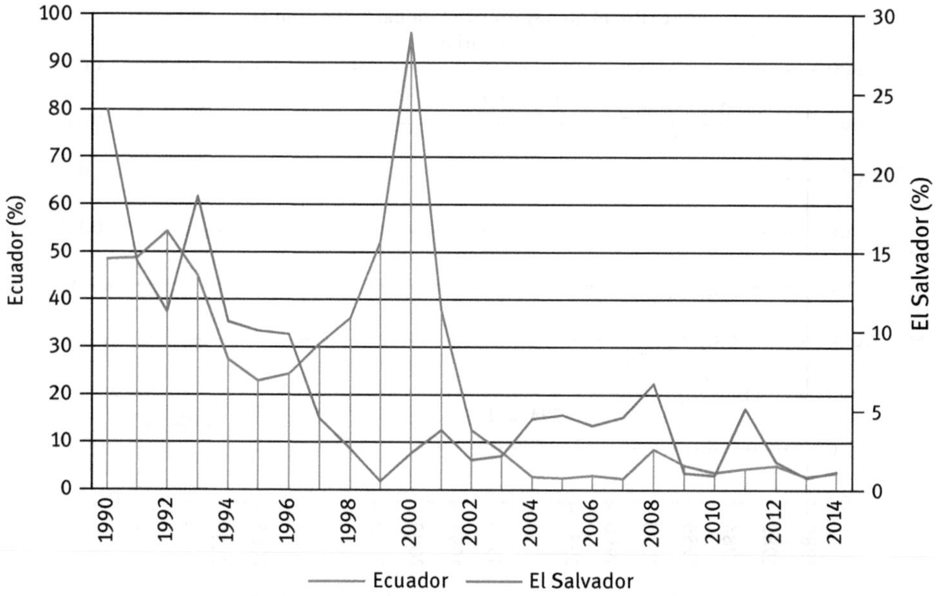

Figure 2.1: Inflation rates in Ecuador and El Salvador.
Source: World Bank.

2.2.2 Fiscal Discipline

Another advantage of full dollarization is that it eliminates the seigniorage option for politicians to finance fiscal deficits. Seigniorage refers to government's revenue generation through creating money; it is a relatively inexpensive method of raising funds for monetary authorities. The elimination of seigniorage encourages fiscal discipline as policy makers can no longer rely on revenue raised from printing more currency, thus have to find new sources of revenue or cut spending to balance their budgets. In the long run, this fosters budgetary discipline—much needed in developing economies.

Note that "printing" money is regarded as one of the causes of high and chronic inflationary processes in many Latin American countries (Peru 1987–1990, for example). Figure 2.2 shows the clear relationship between printing money and inflation in Peru.

2.2.3 Reduction in the Cost of Borrowing

Another benefit of full dollarization is that it not only reduces inflation rates, but also depresses interest rates in the economy as a result. Lower interest rates mean lower financing costs for the government, corporations and households.

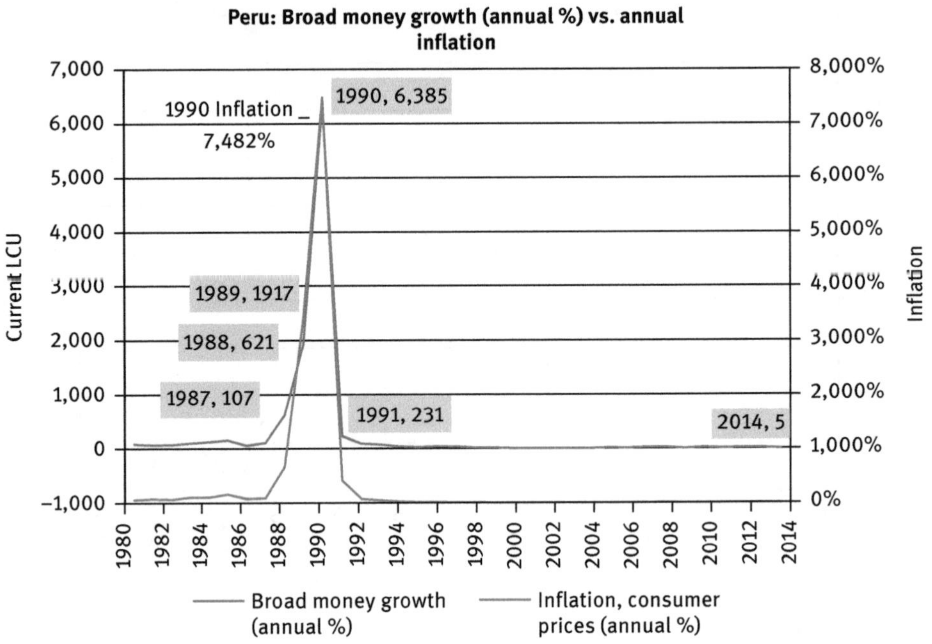

Figure 2.2: Broad money growth and inflation in Peru.
Source: World Bank.

With full dollarization, eliminating the risk of devaluation induces more capital inflows as foreign investors regard the economy as more stable (at least in exchange rate terms). For instance, following its adoption of the US dollar in 2000, Ecuador saw FDI inflows increase from a negative $23 million in 2000 to over $530 million in 2001. The average annual FDI flow into the Ecuadorian economy between 2001 and 2013 was $574.6 million. Net portfolio flows into Ecuador—less than a million dollars in 2000—reached almost $9 million by 2003. Between 2001 and 2013 Ecuador attracted an average net portfolio inflow of $2.1 million (Figure 2.3).

However, it is important to note that even though full dollarization eliminates exchange rate risk, other types of risk such as sovereign and external risks remain. Ultimately, investors consider both types of risk, along with a plethora of other variables, when reaching an investment decision.

2.2.4 Lower Transaction Costs

Full dollarization enables countries to increase the volume of international trade with their main trading partners. In this regard, a country chooses to adopt the currency of

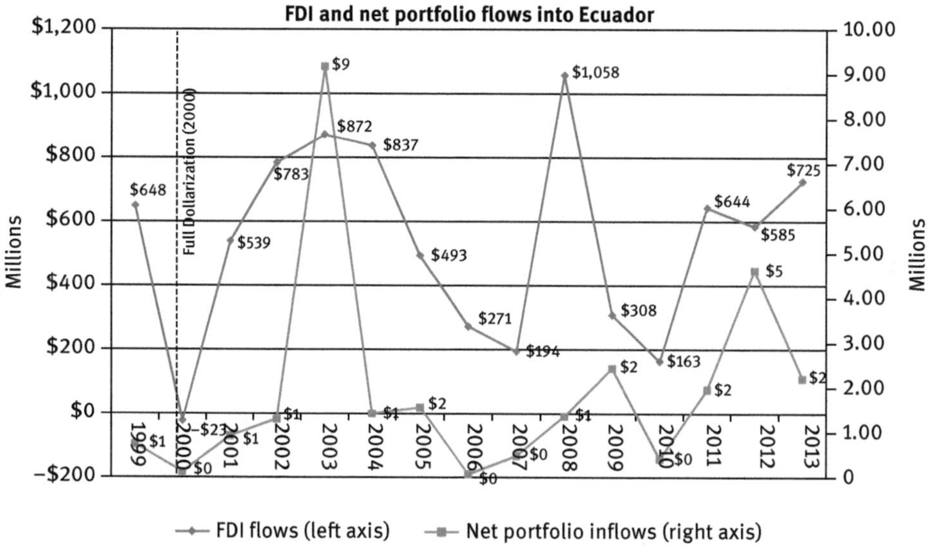

Figure 2.3: FDI flows into Ecuador.
Source: World Bank.

its main trading partner (i.e. for Ecuador and El Salvador the US is the main trading partner, while for Montenegro or Andorra, the European Union is the main trading partner) in order to improve the efficiency of trading with these economies. Sharing the same currency eliminates exchange rate volatility and reduces the transaction costs generated by operating in different currencies, for instance, the costs related to exchanging currency (including commissions or exchange rate spreads) or conducting hedges against currency risk.

As discussed by Rose (1999), sharing a common currency increases the trade between two or more countries to a volume higher than would be the case with different currencies. We can observe this in Figure 2.4, which examines trade between Ecuador and the US. Following the adoption of the dollar in the previous year, trade with the US—around $1 billion in 2000—increased by almost 40% in one year to $1.4 billion in 2001.

By reducing the costs of borrowing and lowering transaction costs, full dollarization not only helps improve the efficiency and volume of trade between economies, but also helps provide non-tradable firms with more stable import prices and lower capital costs. Facilitating non-tradable businesses to grow also has a positive impact on the labor market and helps contribute to stable macroeconomic growth, provided other factors improve at the same time (strong institutions, for example).

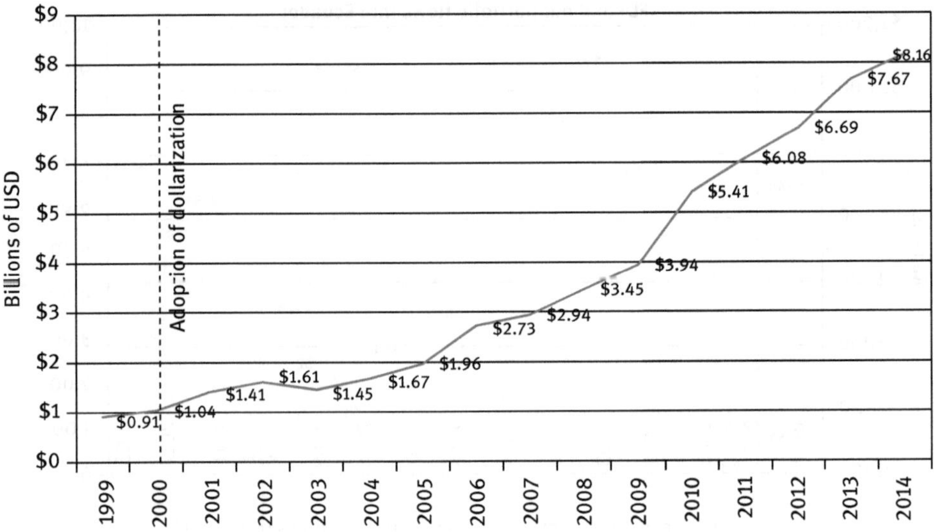

Figure 2.4: US trade with Ecuador.
Source: US Census.

2.3 Benefits of Partial Dollarization

Partial Dollarization is a de facto, gradual process of switching to a foreign currency rather than an official and full switch to a foreign currency. As explained earlier, the factors and precedents that cause partial dollarization to occur differ between economies. However, some common causes include high and chronic inflation (i.e. the loss of local currency's function as a store of value), the loss of trust in the country's institutions and the optimization of agents' foreign and local currency portfolios.

In what follows, we present the benefits of partial dollarization.

2.3.1 Encourages Saving

As explained earlier, one of the most common causes of partial dollarization in an economy is the occurrence of high and chronic inflation. In an economy where the local currency continually loses its value, agents turn to other liquid means to preserve their purchasing power. One of these available options is holding foreign currencies. By providing an alternative to local currency, foreign currency allows economic actors to accrue savings, in the form of a currency that is shielded from local inflationary forces. Allowing foreign currency denominated deposit accounts in the banking system further enables these foreign currency holdings to be channeled into

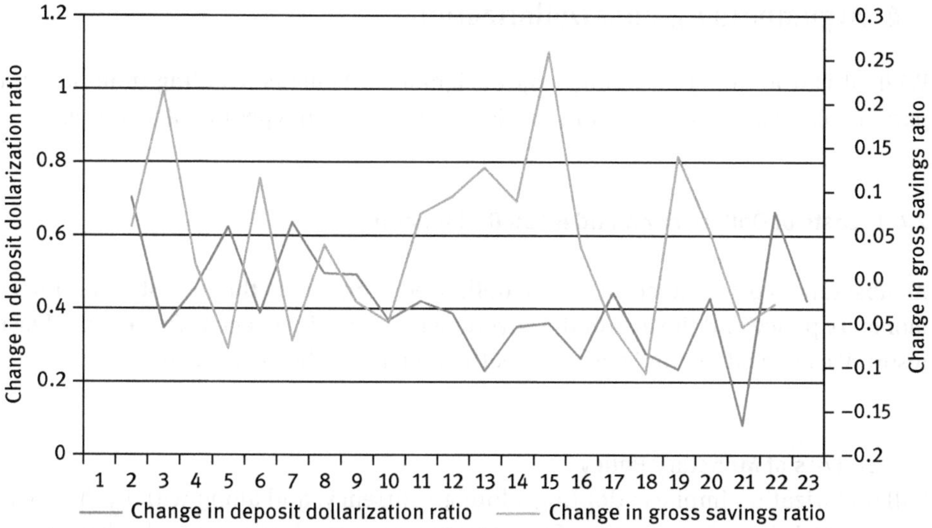

Figure 2.5: Change in gross savings ratio and change in deposit dollarization ratio—Peru (1992–2013).
Source: Author's calculations, Central Bank of Peru, World Bank.

the local economy. Foreign currency accounts also help prevent capital flight, as local savers no longer have to take their savings outside their country. Figure 2.5 shows changes in the deposit dollarization ratio in Peru vs the change in the gross domestic ratio between 1992 and 2013. The two variables appear to be closely correlated.

2.3.2 Promotes Financial Deepening

The desire of economic agents to protect their asset values in terms of purchasing power is another reason for dollarization to take hold. In economies with high and chronic inflation, agents see other currencies as a higher quality investment and sell the local currency to buy foreign currencies. Several agents are able to open accounts outside their countries, yet the vast majority simply dollarize their economies through buying US dollars or other more stable currencies.

One way to prevent capital flight is to allow banks to accept deposits in foreign currencies. Allowing foreign currency accounts increases the volume of savings in an economy (as explained in the previous section). In return, these savings allow banks to extend credit to businesses and consumers, enabling firms to expand, consumers to spend and eventually generating economic growth. From this perspective, we argue that partial dollarization is a promoter of financial deepening in an economy.

Various studies have empirically confirmed this link, and we will explore this effect in greater detail in Chapter 5.

2.4 Arguments Against Dollarization

While it is true that an economy enjoys significant benefits resulting from full and partial dollarization, a significant cost is attached to both types of dollarization.

2.4.1 Costs of Dollarization under Full Dollarization

A substantial cost suffered in a fully dollarized economy is the loss of control over monetary policy and the loss of the government's capacity to act as the lender of last resort. We proceed to briefly describe both problems in the next section.

2.4.1.1 Loss of Monetary Policy

Full dollarization implies adopting a foreign currency, and along with it, the interest rate and the inflation rate of the adopted currency's economy. As the central bank of a fully dollarized economy discontinues issuing its currency, it loses one of its fundamental functions—monetary policy. This means that in the event of external shocks to the economy, the government is limited to using fiscal policy as a response.

2.4.1.2 Inability to Act as a Lender of Last Resort

One of the main functions of a central bank is to act as the lender of last resort to the banking system in times of economic uncertainty or crisis. In fully dollarized economies, the monetary authority loses its ability to provide liquidity to the banking system due to its inability to directly affect the supply of the adopted currency. Under full dollarization, monetary authorities have to find new sources of liquidity for the banking system since printing money is no longer a policy option. Among possible alternative solutions is finding external lines of credit (such as the IMF) that can be used when facing liquidity problems.

2.4.2 Costs of Dollarization under Partial Dollarization

Some of the issues discussed above do not apply to partially dollarized economies. Central banks still maintain control over their monetary policy (albeit in a weaker form) and can continue to act as the lender of last resort. However, partial dollarization puts other restrictions on policy makers. Among these, we can mention the increased foreign exchange risk for the banking system, timing mismatch risks that arise from the maturities of foreign currency loans and deposits in the banking system and an increased default risk that could arise from the fact that banks can extend loans to businesses and households in partially dollarized economies where earnings are not indexed to a foreign currency.

Additionally, conducting monetary policy in partially dollarized economies is more challenging for policymakers, especially when they face external shocks that put pressure on the exchange rate. We will now be looking at each one of these disadvantages in more detail.

2.4.2.1 Increased Foreign Exchange Rate Risk for the Banking System

Banks operating in partially dollarized economies face unique challenges, arising from the fact that their balance sheets contain assets and liabilities in more than one currency. This means the local currency equivalent value of banks' assets and liabilities may change as a result of exchange rate fluctuations.

The existence of this risk compels banks to perform hedging strategies, for example, using derivative market instruments such as swaps. However, this increases costs, which are generally transferred to banking clients in the form of higher interest rates. Banks can hedge their foreign currency deposits by lending in a foreign currency. However, as we describe below, this strategy shifts their currency risk into default risk.

2.4.2.2 Mismatch of Foreign Currency Assets and Liabilities

For a bank, deposits are generally short-term instruments, while assets (credit and loans) have longer maturities. Banks usually hedge risks resulting from mismatch of maturities by using swaps and other derivative instruments. However, in partially dollarized economies, where banks face mismatch risks in more than one currency, such hedging options may not be readily available or may be too expensive for the bank to utilize. As a result, banks in these economies might carry an inherent risk of maturity mismatches between foreign currency denominated assets and liabilities that is difficult to resolve.

2.4.2.3 Increased Default Risk

In conjunction with the currency risks mentioned above, partial dollarization leads banks in partially dollarized banking systems to extend loans in foreign currencies. Banks use these loans in an effort to hedge against currency risks that could arise from holding foreign currency liabilities. However, if foreign currency denominated loans are extended to businesses and households that earn their incomes in a local currency, this hedge is only partial. In the event of devaluations or sharp depreciations of the local currency, the balances of foreign currency loans in local currency

Table 2.3: Example of an increase in default risk as a result of a foreign currency loan.

	Initial conditions	10% depreciation	20% depreciation
Loan in USD	100	100	100
Exchange rate (Pesos/USD)	1	1.1	1.2
Monthly interest rate	5%	5%	5%
Loan duration (months)	4	4	4
Monthly payment in USD	USD 28.20	USD 28.20	USD 28.20
Monthly payment in USD	Pesos 28.20	Pesos 31.02	Pesos 33.84

terms increase, and borrowers who have earnings indexed to local currencies might face difficulties in repayment. For the banking system, this means that currency risk is translated into default risk.

To better understand this, assume that a given household earns 1,000 pesos, that the exchange rate is 1 peso per dollar and that the household has a 4-month, 100 dollar loan with a 5% compounded monthly interest rate. A sudden and persistent depreciation of 10% increases the local currency value of the household's dollar denominated loan (it increases its loan cost from 5% to 9.23%). With this increase, each payment now represents 31% of the household's income (versus 28.2% before the devaluation). Table 2.3 presents the results of this example.

A 20% depreciation is equivalent to an interest rate increase from 5% to 13.32%, and repayments as a percentage of household income jump from 28.2% to 33.84%.[1] This simple example also shows the impact of volatility in exchange rates on loan payments.

2.4.2.4 Monetary Policy Challenges

While under full dollarization, the authorities lose their monetary policy apparatus; in partially dollarized economies a more complicated challenge awaits regulators and central bankers. In a partially dollarized economy, the money supply includes more than one currency. When formulating exchange rate and monetary policies, central bankers have to pay attention to exchange rate fluctuations (volatility).

1 The payment can be estimated using the PMT command in excel or using a financial calculator. The increase in interest rate is calculated using the IRR command. Excel file used for this example is available upon request. Mathematically, the payments are estimated using the annuity formula:

$$PMT = PV\left(\frac{(1+i)^n xi}{(1+i)^n - 1}\right)$$

Lowering the monetary policy rate might stimulate the economy, but this action can also depreciate the value of the local currency,[2] increasing the local currency balances of foreign currency denominated loans in the banking system. In return, this depreciation may create hardship for borrowers holding foreign currency loans, increasing the number of debtors who will default. These defaulted loans accumulate on bank balance sheets as toxic assets, placing the economy in peril.

Alternatively, raising the monetary policy rate can make the local currency stronger by attracting capital flows into the economy. A stronger local currency can encourage borrowers to choose foreign currency loans as opposed to local currency loans, thereby increasing foreign currency lending in the banking system.[3]

Given the risks involved with a fluctuating currency, some dollarized economies prefer to follow fixed exchange rate regimes where the central bank pegs the value of the local currency to a single foreign currency or a basket of foreign currencies. This regime requires sufficiently large foreign reserves to prop up the exchange rate, and strict fiscal and monetary discipline on the part of the authorities. The East Asian Financial crisis is a good case study on how artificially overvalued local currencies can lead to problems for the central bank authorities.

An alternative to pegged regimes is a free float system enhanced with an appropriate monetary policy or inflation targeting regime. Under such a scenario, policy makers have to identify the role of foreign currency deposits as they choose their monetary policy targets. (Quispe-Agnoli, 2002). Empirical evidence has illustrated that deposit dollarization tends to be more pronounced (more so than credit dollarization) in economies with floating exchange rate regimes (Arteta, 2005).

Which exchange rate regime works best with dollarization is still debated among economists. The focus of this debate centers on the question of how institutions hedge the exchange and default risks mentioned earlier. While some studies (such as Burnside, Eichenbaum and Rebelo, 2001; Goldstein, 2002) show that fixed exchange rate regimes discourage hedging by financial institutions in a dollarized economy, since there is an implicit guarantee that the central monetary authority would defend the exchange rate no matter what, other research (such as McKinnon 2000; Arteta, 2005)

---

2 Normally, when central banks decrease their monetary policy rates, local interest rates also decrease. In terms of portfolio investments, this makes the risk premium increase and leads investors to cut local investments from their portfolios. Consequently, large quantities of a foreign currency such as dollars are demanded, and the price (in terms of local currency) increases (depreciates). If central governments believe this is a temporary shock they usually intervene in foreign exchange markets by providing the necessary liquidity using their international reserves. This is something that has been observed during the last few years in several countries, e.g. Peru and Colombia.

3 Ozsoz, Rengifo and Kutan (2015) has found evidence in the Turkish banking system that foreign currency lending by the banking system increases during periods of appreciation of the local currency. This happens due to a perception amongst borrowers that loans denominated in foreign currencies are cheap.

shows that under floating exchange rate regimes, the cost of hedging would be greater than in a fixed exchange rate system, thus fewer banks would hedge. This second view suggests that currency mismatch risks are greater in floating exchange rate regimes. In support of this view, other studies (such as Berg and Borensztein, 2000) illustrated that the adoption of a floating exchange rate regime may result in higher volatility in the exchange rate, since shifts in money demand would likely be sizeable in dollarized economies. Individual country studies (such as Ozsoz, Rengifo and Kutan, 2015) support this perspective. For instance, in the case of Turkey, a floating exchange rate regime does not necessarily reduce the amount of risk in the banking system. For almost every 100 Turkish lira equivalent of foreign currency deposited in the banking system, the equivalent of 70 lira was lent out by the banking system between the fourth quarter of 2002 and the second quarter of 2009. We investigate this relationship in more detail in Chapter 4 where we discuss the impact of dollarization in banking systems.

3 What Causes Dollarization?

3.1 Introduction

As mentioned in Chapter 1, there are various reasons as to why dollarization takes hold in an economy. Our aim in this chapter is to highlight some of the main causes of partial dollarization across different regions and specific countries around the world.

We start the chapter by introducing the theoretical link between inflation and dollarization while highlighting the importance of exchange rate movements as a determinant of dollarization and explaining the transmission mechanism through which exchange rates are passed onto inflation. In line with the inflation and dollarization argument, we then analyze currency substitution theory, using empirical evidence drawn from literature and from the behavior of dollarized economies. In Section 3.3, we introduce the idea of "De-dollarization Hysteresis" and delineate the new ideas that aim to explain the phenomenon. Two important emerging theories of De-dollarization Hysteresis—Minimum Variance Portfolio Theory and the Institutions Argument—are covered in Section 3.4.

3.2 Inflation and Dollarization

Early literature examining dollarization (also known as the currency substitution theory) focused on the effect of inflation on dollarization. The currency substitution theory states that interest rate differentials among countries are predictors of foreign currency holdings.

The theory is based on the expected interest rate parity between local and foreign currency interest rates. Accordingly, (current[1]) local currency interest rates should be equal to those paid on foreign currency balances plus an expected rate of depreciation of the local currency:

$$i_l^c = (1+i_f)(1+i_{dep})-1 \tag{3.1}$$

Where i_l^c represents the current local interest rate, i_f the foreign interest rate and i_{dep} the depreciation rate. In real terms the interest rate is given by:

$$i_l^r = \frac{(1+i_f)(1+i_{dep})}{1+\pi} - 1 \tag{3.2}$$

1 Recall that interest rates can be expressed in terms of nominal or current values and in real terms, by considering the effects of inflation (purchasing power). Nominal interest rates do not take into consideration the effects of inflation, while real interest rates do.

Where i_l^r represents the real local interest rate and π represents the local inflation rate. Reordering Eq. (3.2), we get:

$$i_l^r = \frac{(1+i_f)(1+i_{dep})-1-\pi}{1+\pi} \rightarrow i_l^r = \frac{i_l^c-\pi}{1+\pi} \tag{3.3}$$

In order to show the relationship between the inflation rate and the depreciation rate, we rewrite Eq. (3.2) and obtain the following relationship:

$$i_{dep} = \frac{(1+i_l^r)(1+\pi)}{1+i_f} - 1 \tag{3.4}$$

Equation (3.4) tells us that increases in the inflation rate are correlated with increases in the (expected) rate of depreciation in the local currency, assuming fixed local and foreign interest rates.

Figure 3.1 presents the relationship between dollarization of banks' liabilities and the inflation rates for several selected countries (Argentina, Brazil, Bulgaria, Korea, Poland, Romania, Russian Federation, Slovak Republic, South Africa, Turkey,

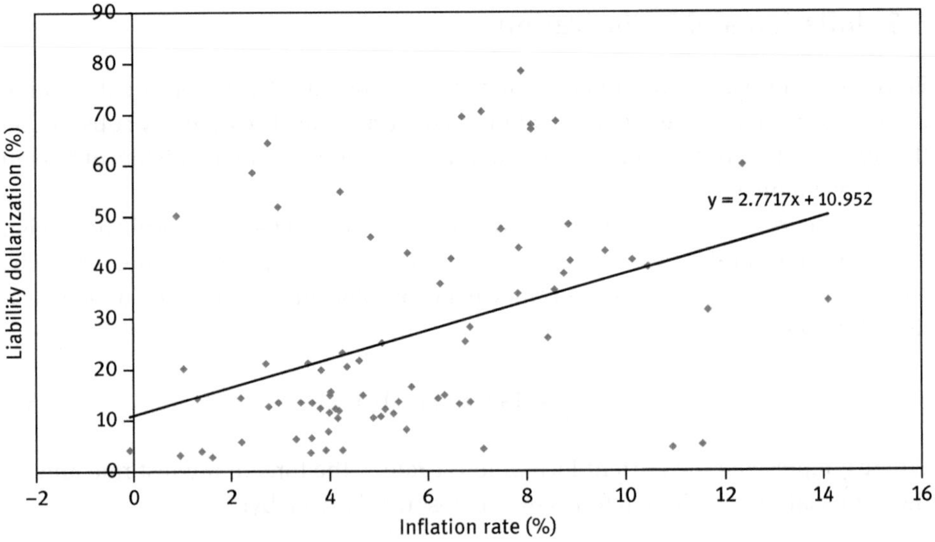

Figure 3.1: Liability dollarization and inflation.
Figure 3.1 shows liability dollarization ratios for selected low inflation economies (Argentina, Brazil, Bulgaria, Korea, Poland, Romania, Russian Federation, Slovak Republic, South Africa, Turkey, Uruguay and Mexico between 2005 and 2013) versus the inflation rate.
Source: World Bank, IMF IFS. The equation for the linear trend line is: Liability Dollarization = 2.7717 Inflation Rate = 10.952.

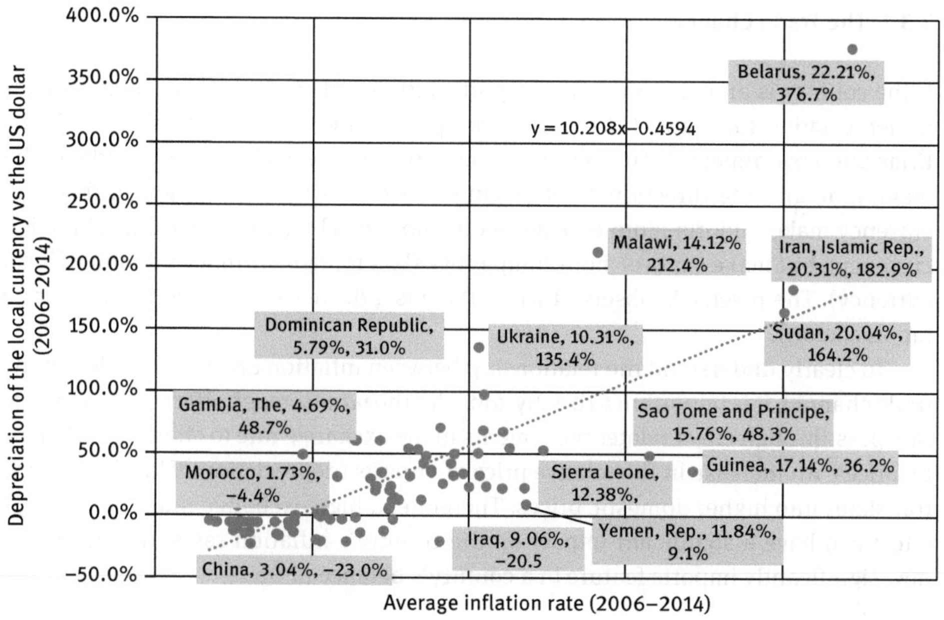

Figure 3.2: Depreciation and inflation.
Figure 3.2 shows depreciation of the local currency versus the US dollar and the average inflation rate between 2006 and 2014 for 102 low, middle and lower middle income countries.
Source: World Bank, The equation for the linear trend line is: Depreciation vs. the US Dollar = 10.208 Average Inflation = 0.459.

Uruguay and Mexico). From this figure, we can infer two facts: firstly, the higher the inflation rate is, the higher the dollarization in liabilities becomes. Secondly, the higher the dollarization of banks' liabilities is, the higher is the exposure to default risk in the case of serious and permanent currency depreciations.

Local currency depreciations transmitted to the real economy via the country's terms of trade and via their impact on local financial markets. Figure 3.2 illustrates this relationship. The average inflation rates for the 102 low and middle-income countries are plotted against the average depreciation rate of these countries' currencies between 2006 and 2014. We can observe from the shape of the linear trend line that there is a positive and direct relationship between inflation and depreciation of the local currency in these economies.

3.3 Transmission Mechanisms

We can distinguish several mechanisms that explain the relationships between exchange rate movements and inflation. In this section, we present three mechanisms: the trade, credit and liability channels.

3.3.1 The Trade Channel

If the country is an open economy (imports and exports are allowed), then changes in depreciation rates affect the purchasing power of economic agents (individuals, firms and governments). The degree of the impact of these changes depends on the magnitude and the direction of the change. Increases in depreciation of the local currency make imports more expensive (i.e. more local currency per unit of foreign currency), but make exports more competitive (less foreign currency per unit of local currency). The reverse is observed when there is a decrease in the depreciation rate (appreciation).

To clearly understand the relationship between inflation and dollarization in the trade channel, it is important to briefly consider the *pass-through* effect. The exchange rate pass-through effect relates movements in the exchange rate to changes in domestic prices. An increase in the relative price of imports (depreciation of local currency) translates into higher domestic prices. Therefore, a high exchange rate pass-through effect can have a significant impact on the country's inflation rates, depending on how significantly imports feature in a country's balance of trade.

3.3.2 The Credit Channel

The credit channel transmission mechanism concerns how changes in exchange rates also affect financial markets. Among many other variables, the degree to which this mechanism impacts upon financial markets depends on the level of financial development and dollarization of the economy in question.

Empirical and theoretical studies have shown that economies with developed financial systems are more resilient to economic shocks. (For more on financial development and economic resilience, see Bernanke, Gertler, and Gilchrist, 1999, among others.)[2]

Additionally, sophisticated financial markets enable credit expansion, thus contributing to economic growth. King and Levine (1993) produced one of the first studies on the subject, which showed in a cross-country regression that initial levels of financial depth (measured by the by the size of the banking system relative to GDP) leads to growth rates over time when controlled for other explanatory variables. Other research has shown that financial deepening over the long run is an important catalyst for economic growth in emerging markets (see Darrat, Elkhal and McCallum, 2006).

---

2 However, more recently Sahay et al. (2015) illustrated that this relationship is not linear, meaning that "Financial development initially lowers growth volatility, as it allows for an expansion of opportunities for effective risk management and diversification. After a certain point, volatility begins to increase." (p. 21).

The impact of dollarization on financial deepening has also been the subject of recent empirical research. Court, Ozsoz and Rengifo (2012) tested the effect of deposit dollarization on the financial deepening of these economies by using a battery of models. Their findings suggest that dollarization has a consistent and significant negative effect on the financial deepening of economies in their sample.[3] Research results also suggest that in high inflationary economies, dollarization has a moderating effect on inflation. These findings are also consistent at the regional level.

3.3.3 Liability Channel

Related to the credit channel, the liability channel shows the relationship between depreciation (appreciation), dollarization and its impact on agents' liabilities. The basic idea is that if individuals have loans in foreign currency and earn incomes in local currency, an increase in depreciation rates has a negative impact on their ability to repay their debts (more of the local currency is required to buy the foreign currency needed to pay for the foreign-denominated loans). Moreover, from the point of view of an agent that has savings in local currency, an increase in depreciation rates implies that the real value of his savings decrease, since in general, local interest rates react very slowly to adjust for changes in local moneys.

In order to illustrate the transmission effect of the liabilities channel mechanism, Figure 3.3 shows the depreciation of local currencies for several Latin American countries (Argentina, Brazil, Chile, Colombia, Paraguay, Peru, Uruguay and Venezuela). The figure presents the changes in local currencies per US dollars. The year selected was 2013, which was selected as a base in order to show the speed at which local currencies can depreciate.

Figure 3.3 shows that since January 2014, most Latin American Countries have experienced significant depreciations of their local currencies. For example, by the end of October 2015, the Peruvian currency depreciated 26% with respect to its

3 The economists used a sample of 44 dollarized economies for the 1996–2002 period. For financial deepening measure, the authors used credit-to-GDP ratio which is available from IMF's International Financial Statistics (IFS) database. As for the dollarization variable the authors mainly used the ratio of foreign currency deposits to total deposits in the banking system. For robustness checks, the authors also used the ratio of foreign currency deposits in the banking system to the M2 money supply. The amount of foreign exchange deposits in the banking system is obtained from Central Bank bulletins. For countries and years for which the data is not available from the CB bulletins, the authors used the foreign currency deposit database compiled by Levy-Yeyati (2006). The authors also use institutional quality variables as instruments in their estimations. Creditor Rights Index (CRI) and Private Credit Bureau Availability Dummy (PB) are obtained from World Bank's Doing Business website. The authors employ two econometric models in their analysis using OLS and TSLS techniques.

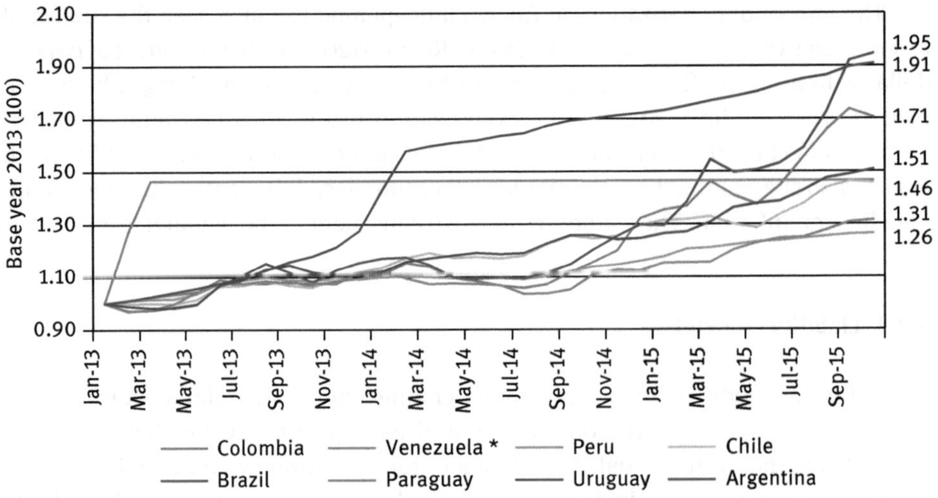

Figure 3.3: Currency depreciation for Latin American countries (2013–2015).
Figure 3.3 shows the depreciation of local currencies per US dollar for several Latin American Countries (Argentina, Brazil, Chile, Colombia, Paraguay, Peru, Uruguay and Venezuela). The base year selected was 2013.

January 2013 value (2.55–3.22 Nuevos Soles per US dollar). Taking the Peruvian case, a 1,000 USD loan in January 2013 was equivalent to 2,550 Nuevos Soles, and by the end of October 2015, the same 1,000 USD loan was equivalent to 3,220 Nuevos Soles—in real terms, a 26% increase in the loan's cost in a little under 3 years.

Figure 3.4 shows the depreciation of four Eastern European currencies (the Czech Koruna, the Hungarian Forint, Polish Zloty and the Russian Ruble). One can easily observe that the Russian Ruble has experienced the most loss in its value in the sample, dropping from 30.2 rubles per USD in January 2013 to as little as 65 Rubles per USD in October 2015. In the meantime, the other three currencies experienced depreciations significantly below the Ruble, averaging a 20% loss in value over the same period.

In Figure 3.5 we can see the depreciations of some of the African currencies versus the US dollar since January 2013. Among the eight currencies used in the comparison, the Zambian Kwacha and the Ghanaian Cedi depreciated the most versus the US Dollar during the two-year timeframe. In the meantime, average depreciation of the remaining six currencies (West African Franc, Kenyan and Tanzanian Shilling, South African Rand, Nigerian Naira and Mozambique Meticai) has been around 30% over the same period.

From Figures 3.4 and 3.5, one can appreciate the obvious grave effect that this depreciation has on economic agents' liabilities (see the Peruvian example presented above).

Of course, local currency depreciations also create problems for banks. As mentioned previously, banks try to minimize currency mismatches arising from

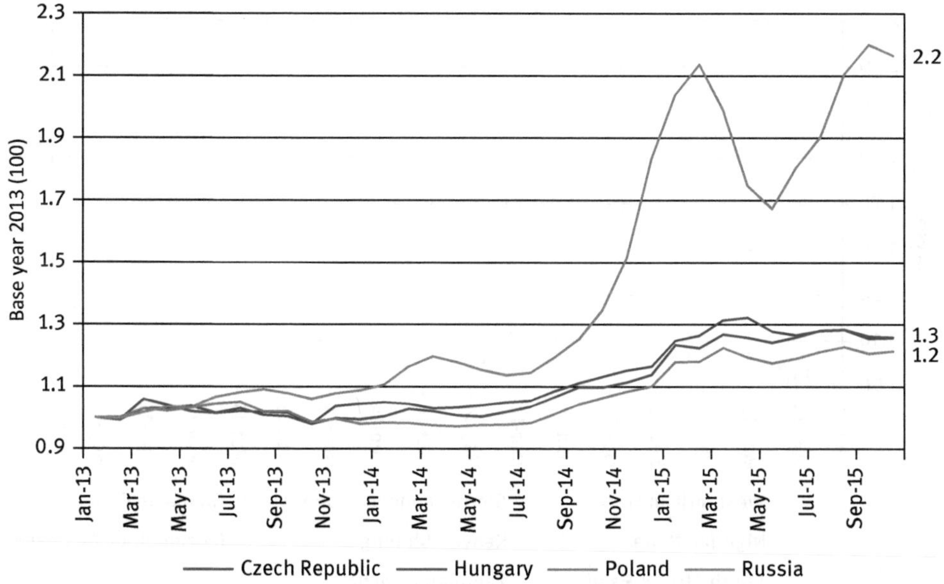

Figure 3.4: Currency depreciation for selected eastern European countries (2013–2015). Figure 3.4 shows the depreciation of local currencies per US dollar for several Eastern European countries (Czech Republic, Hungary, Poland and Russia). The base year selected was 2013. Source: World Bank Databank.

dollar-denominated deposits by issuing dollar-denominated loans. However, under depreciation pressures, having large dollar-denominated loans simply increases banks' default risks.

Continuing with the Peruvian case, its Central Bank tried to reduce the Nuevos Soles depreciation pressure against the US dollar by constant open market operations (selling in their US dollar denominated international reserves in the open market). The results presented in Figure 3.3 showed their inability to do so. The central bank's failure to stabilize exchange rates can be attributed to the idea that central governments interventions are only effective to fight short term foreign exchange movements (volatility) and not long-term, fundamental changes in the market; for example, the recent changes observed during 2014–2015 (Ostry, Ghosh and Chamon, 2012).[4]

4 During these years, commodity prices (mainly mineral and oil related) fell dramatically due to a slowdown in China's economy. Along with this slowdown, China's demand for imports from several Latin American countries fell. US Fed rates uncertainties are clearly signals of market unpredictability, that cannot be remedied through government action alone.

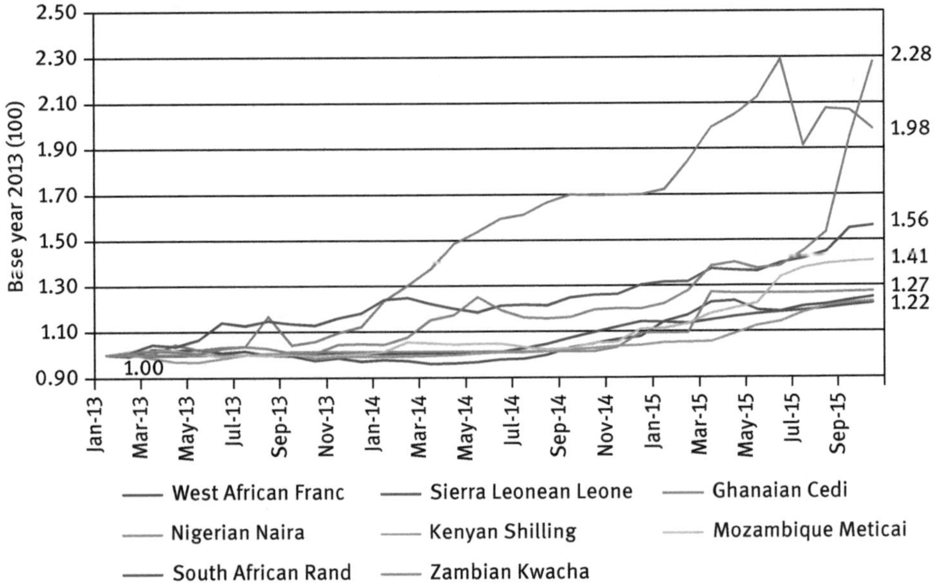

Figure 3.5: Currency depreciation for selected African economies (2013–2015).
Figure 3.5 shows the depreciation of several African currencies (Ghanaian Cedi, West African Franc, Kenyan Shilling, South African Rand, Sierra Leonean Leone, Nigerian Naira, Mozambique Meticais and Zambian Kwacha) per US dollar. The base year selected was 2013.
Source: World Bank Databank.

Figure 3.6, presents this information in terms of the fluctuation of net international reserves between January 2013 and October 2015. This figure shows the central bank's efforts to avoid the observed depreciation by using its foreign exchange reserves to prop up the market. In years previous to those presented in the figures, the Peruvian central bank had had a very successful track record of open market interventions that allowed them to significantly reduce exchange rate volatility. However, the interventions during the last couple of years have proven to be unsuccessful due to the new state of the global economic environment, where changes appear to be of a more permanent nature (commodity prices have decreased for the foreseeable medium and long term). In any case, the Peruvian central bank response (as opposed to the Chilean response) appears to be coherent with the high dollarization of the Peruvian economy (as opposed to very low Chilean dollarization).

Large depreciations of local currencies, as explained by the aforementioned transmission mechanisms, and the observed positive relationship between inflation and depreciation explain the natural response of economic agents: increasing their dollarization levels!

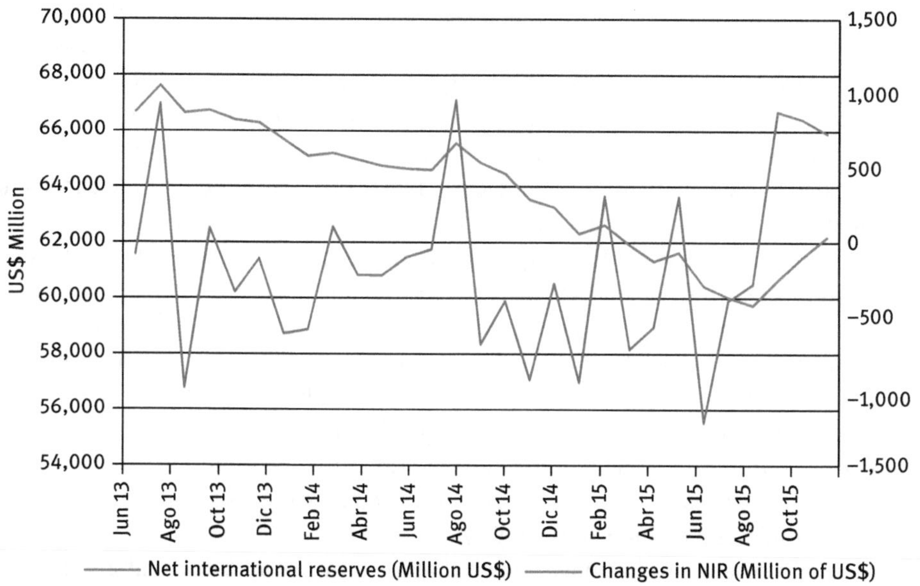

Figure 3.6: Net international reserves, Peru (2013–2015).
Figure 3.6 shows the Peruvian net international reserves and its changes for the period January 2013–October 2015.
Source: Banco Central de Reserva del Perú.

3.3.4 Evidence on Currency Substitution Theory

Evidence on currency substitution theory is mixed. The early contributors to this literature such as Miles (1978), Gilton and Roper (1981) and McKinnon[5] (1982) have shown that when agents hold local and foreign currency in their portfolios, "variations in foreign interest rates or expected future exchange rates can make domestic money demand functions unstable" (Thomas, 1985, p. 347). This is mainly because agents can alter their portfolio holdings in response to changes in relative returns. Girton and Roper list the implications of this theory as follows: Currency Substitution produces "... instability in the sense that shifts in the anticipated rate of exchange rate change produce larger movements in the exchange rate and these movements are unbounded as [currency substitution] CS increases." Another implication is that "... if two monies are perfect substitutes in demand, their rate of exchange is indeterminate" (p. 26).

5 McKinnon's seminal work on currency substitution published in the American Economic review in 1982 is one of the first papers that developed this theory. McKinnon pointed out the complications of foreign currency substitutability in managing domestic money supply (McKinnon, 1982).

The idea gained traction among economists as more literature, such as the studies produced by Thomas (1985), Cuddington et al. (1989), Vegh (1992) and Savastano (1996), focused on the idea. Some early empirical studies have provided support for the currency substitution theory. Among these studies, we can mention Ramirez-Rojas' work (1985), which observed the magnitude of currency substitution in Argentina, Mexico and Uruguay from 1970s to early 1980s and illustrated that the expected change in the exchange rate was an important determinant of currency substation in the three countries.[6] The study recommends that policy makers increase real rates of return on local currencies and contract the local money supply to combat currency substitution. Further empirical evidence produced by Elkhafif (2003) supports these findings, showing that South Africa (which targeted inflation as opposed to using an exchange rate anchor program) was more successful in lowering its currency substitution rates compared to Egypt during the 1990s. In a later study, Eichengreen (2002) shows that countries tackling dollarization will find inflation targeting a more attractive policy, as opposed to the policy of using the exchange rate as an anchor, provided that the central bank maintains credibility.

Although several studies have shown that in countries with high inflation rates currency substitution leads to dollarization, recent experiences of highly dollarized economies following the drop in their inflation levels led many to question the validity or universality of this theory (see section below).

In the next section, we present alternative explanations of the possible causes of dollarization that can better explain the phenomena that have been observed in dollarized economies in recent times.

3.4 De-Dollarization Hysteresis

One of the accepted facts in the dollarization literature is the lack of reversibility of dollarization processes, even after inflation levels decreased to controlled levels. The so-called "ratchet effect" of dollarization has been evidenced in Latin America and Eastern Europe, and has attracted much attention in the dollarization literature since the early 90s (Calvo and Veigh, 1992).

Figure 3.7 provides examples to the so-called de-dollarization hysteresis. As observed, dollarization rates in Turkey (measured by ratio of total foreign currency denominated bank deposits to total deposits) remains relatively high despite the drop in the inflation rate after 2001. The same can be observed in the Russian Federation, Bulgaria, Cambodia, Honduras and Belarus. Inflation in Russia fell from 873% in 2003 to 14% in 2013. During 1993–2003 period however, the dollarization ratio

6 It is important to note that the author makes a special note to the "irreversibility" of the phenomenon in the three countries.

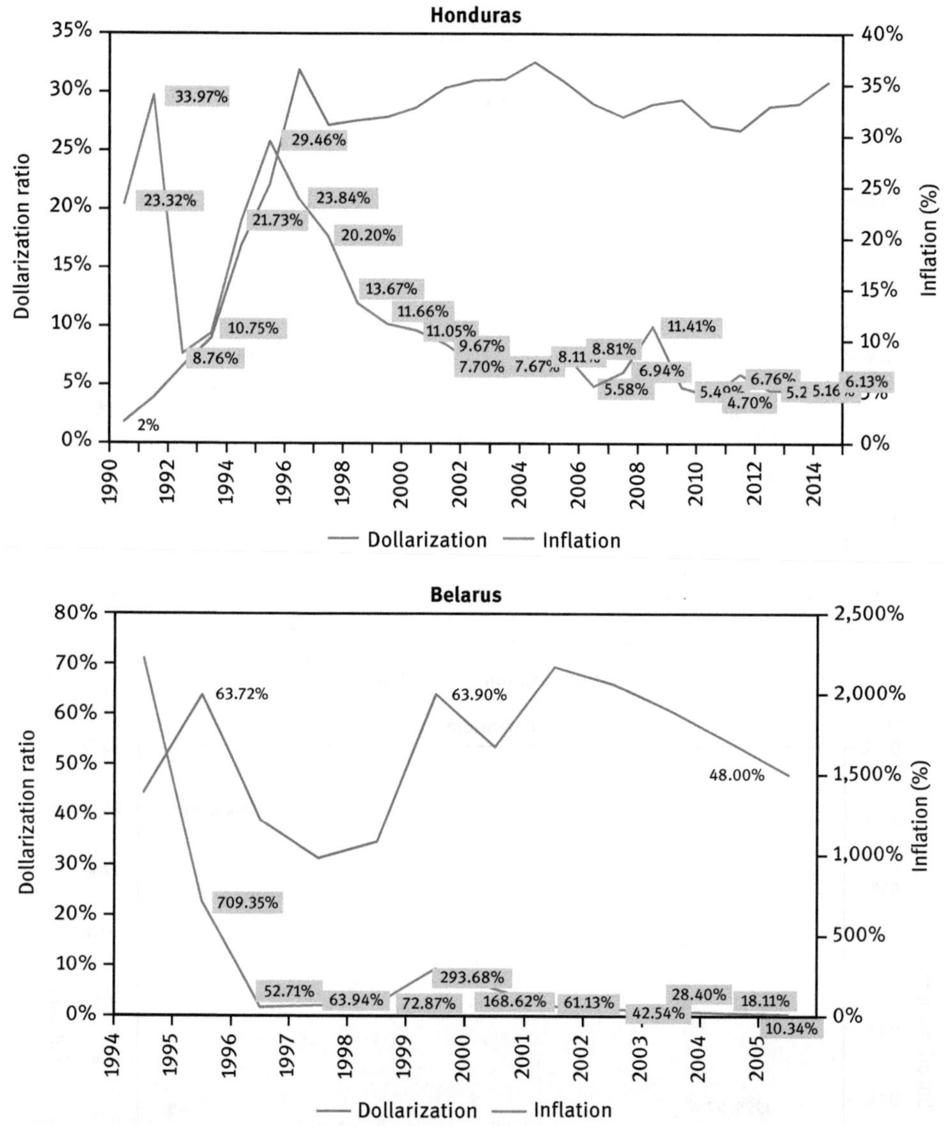

Figure 3.7: Dollarization and inflation in selected economies.

Figure 3.7 show the dollarization ratios and inflation rates in selected dollarized economies including Honduras, Belarus, Turkey, Cambodia, Bulgaria and Russia. The dollarization ratio used is the ratio of foreign currency deposits in the banking system to the total bank deposits.
Source: IMF-IFS, Yeyati (2006) National Bank of Honduras.

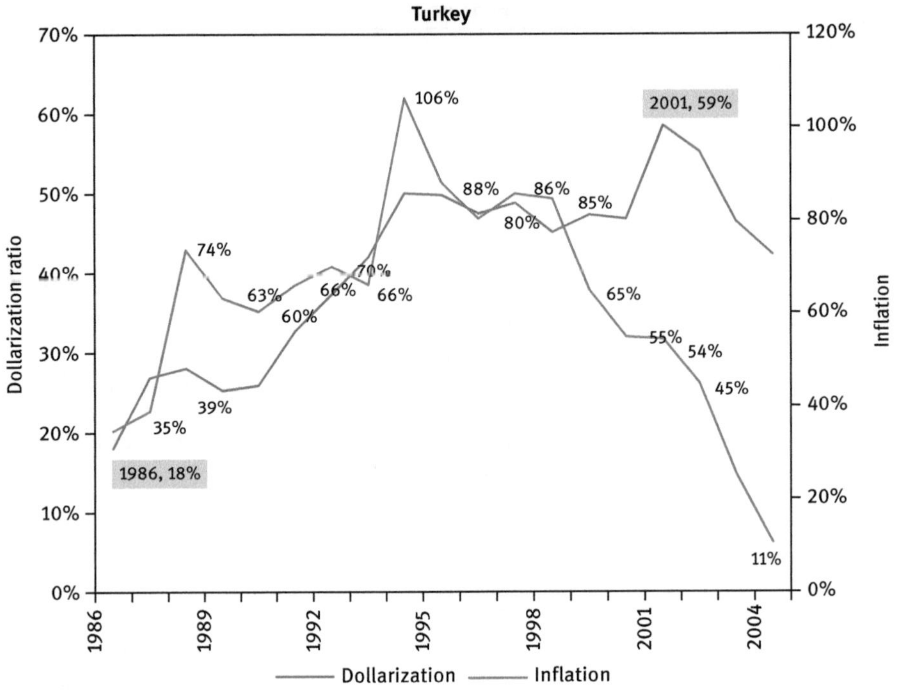

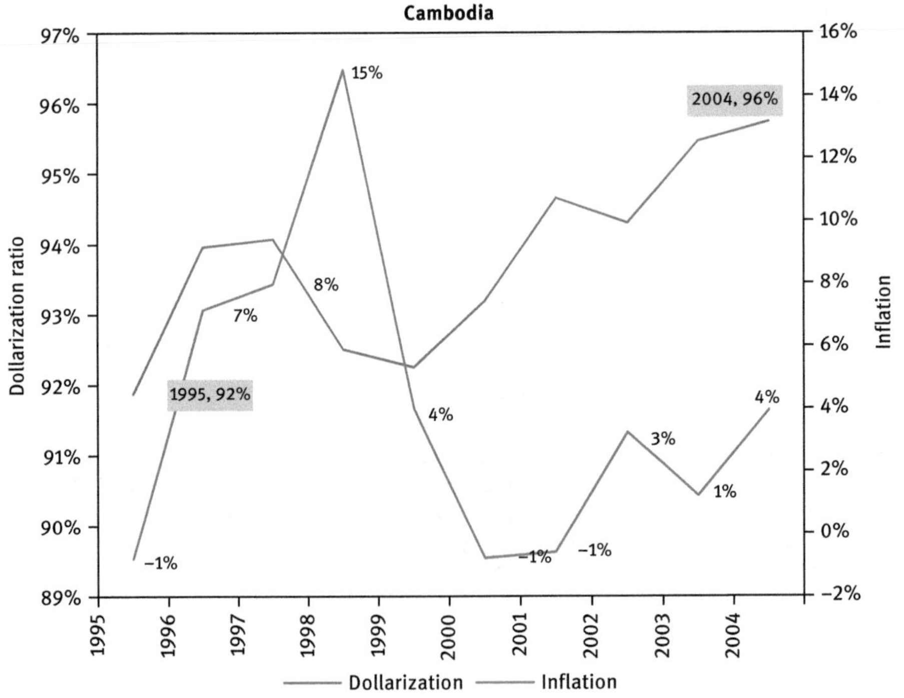

Figure 3.7: (continued)

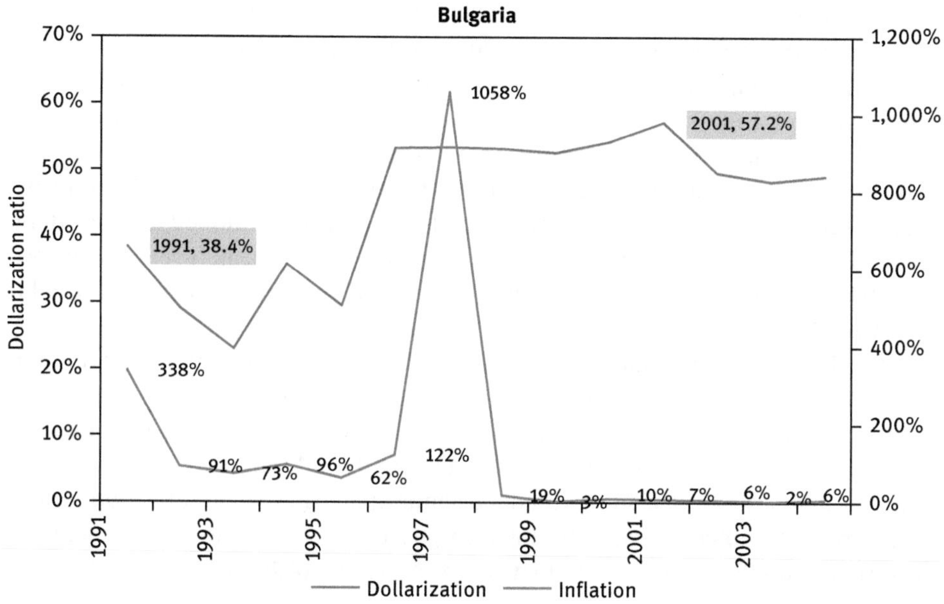

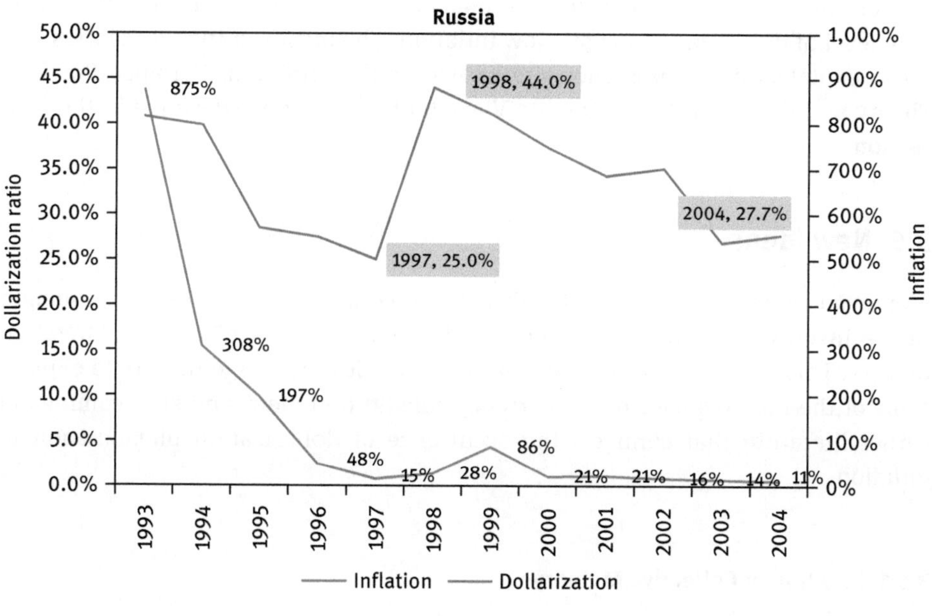

Figure 3.7: (continued)

only fell by 14 percentage points (from 40.8% in 1993 to 26.9% in 2003). In the case of Bulgaria, the dollarization ratio (measured as the ratio of foreign currency deposits in the banking system versus overall deposits) reached a high of 54% in 1997 when country's inflation rate peaked at 1,058%. Although inflation later retreated to 6.35% in 2004, its dollarization ratio remained as high as 49%. Another transition economy, Belarus also suffered from runaway inflation during the 90s. The country's annual inflation rate reached a record high of 2,221% in 1994 and fell to single digits by 2005. However, the dollarization ratio, which reached its peak (over 64%) in 1995 and 1999 (inflation is above 700% and 290% in both years respectively), only fell to 48% by 2005.

Another pertinent example is Cambodia. The country has seen its inflation rate fall from an average of 56% per year between 1990 and 1998 to an average of 3.5% between 1998 and 2004, yet the ratio of foreign currency accounts to total deposits remained over 90%. Honduras, which never saw its inflation rate reach over 34% between 1990 and 2014, also represents a similar pattern. The dollarization ratio in the country remained consistently high despite the fact that the country achieved single digit inflation rates after 2000 (with the exception of 2008, when inflation rose to 11.4%).

Recent literature provides us with plausible explanations for this persistently high level of dollarization despite low inflation. The most significant theories that try to explain this phenomenon are known as the Minimum Variance Portfolio Theory and the Institutional Quality View, both of which we describe in the next section.

3.5 New Ideas

As previously mentioned, despite advances in controlling inflation, one common theme in most dollarized economies is the observed lack of a de-dollarization process. This leaves room for new ideas and theories to emerge that try to explain some of the inefficiencies of the currency substitution view, and shortcomings in earlier literature that connects the occurrence of dollarization phenomenon to inflation.

3.5.1 Inflation in Collective Memory

The "Inflation in Collective Memory" theory offers an explanation as to why de-dollarization does not take place in most countries, despite the successes of the authorities in bringing runaway inflation under control. The damaging effect of inflation upon the socio-economic fabric of society remains in the collective memory of economic agents, who keep dollars in case of future inflationary events.

The so-called “ratchet effect” is hard to reverse once the public accepts the use of substitute currencies in its daily transactions. Mongardini and Mueller (1999)[7] describe this phenomenon as follows:

> In the case of high inflation countries, the ratchet effect was attributed to a costly process of developing, learning and applying strategies to “beat” inflation. Such strategies, commonly labelled as financial innovations, include, inter alia, the rapid switching between demand deposits and savings deposits in domestic currency, the evolution of high yielding or indexed money substitutes, the efficient use of overdrafts, the application of portfolio optimization methods and most notably the flight into foreign currency assets. Over time, an increasing proportion of the public resorts to these forms of financial innovation. The large fixed costs involved in adopting these strategies as well as their wide-spread use and acceptance throughout the economy induce households and enterprises to expand their use of these substitutes even in the event of a decline in inflation or an appreciation of the exchange rate agents become “locked in” the new pattern. Only a significant decline in inflation or a considerable appreciation of the currency can overcome the sunk costs in “inflation-beating” strategies and provide enough incentives for households to eventually revert to traditional domestic money balances. (p. 13)

There are numerous examples of the “ratchet effect” from dollarized economies. As illustrated in Figure 3.7, the decline in inflation rates does not necessarily cause dollarization ratios to fall.

3.5.2 Minimum Variance Portfolio (MVP) Theory

Introduced by A. Ize and E. Levy-Yeyati in their 2003 paper “Financial Dollarization”, the MVP theory is based on a portfolio model of financial intermediation in which currency choice is determined by hedging decisions on both sides of a bank’s balance sheet.

Ize and Yeyati’s approach to the dollarization discussion is from the loan dollarization perspective. Banks that have foreign currency deposits hedge their dollar liabilities by lending in foreign currency or using derivatives. In doing so, banks hedge against foreign exchange rate risk and inflation. The portfolio theory assumes that the interaction between banks’ foreign currency deposits and their foreign currency loans in the loanable funds market gravitates around interest rate parity and minimum variance portfolio allocations. According to this view, the currency composition of the MVP portfolio can be explained by inflation volatility and the depreciation of the local currency in real terms.

For a given variance of inflation, an increase in the “variance of the rate of depreciation reduces dollarization by limiting the hedging benefits of dollar assets”. The authors argue that stabilization policies aimed at reducing inflation rates may fail

7 For a more detailed discussion of the “ratchet effect” see Mongardini and Mueller (1999).

to reduce dollarization rates if the policies also target real rates. This conjecture provides meaningful reasons as to why de-dollarization does not transpire in countries where inflation rates have stabilized.

As several economists explain, in economies where inflation rates are controlled, dollarization can prevail "even when the memory of past macroeconomic imbalances fade away," largely because "the expected volatility of inflation is high in relation to that of the real exchange rate" (p. 326). An important implication of the MVP theory is that countries can reduce dollarization rates if they follow an inflation targeting regime with a freely floating exchange rate. This combination would increase real exchange rate volatility relative to price volatility.[8]

In order to provide a detailed explanation of the mechanisms related to this theory, the next sections present empirical evidence that supports Ize and Levy Yeyati's MVP model.

3.5.2.1 The MVP Model

The model developed by Ize and Levy Yeyati (2003) establishes the assumption that domestic depositors' portfolios are made up of three types of assets: local currency deposits (local), foreign currency deposits (foreign) and foreign currency deposits held outside the country (cross).

The real returns for the three types of assets are r^{local}, $r^{foreign}$, and r^{cross}. Other assumptions include the inability to short-sell any currency and the lack of cash in the portfolio. The real returns in the portfolio are expressed as:

$$r^{local} = E(r^{local}) - \mu_\pi + \mu_c \tag{3.5}$$

$$r^{foreign} = E(r^{foreign}) + \mu_s + \mu_c \tag{3.6}$$

$$r^{cross} = E(r^{cross}) + \mu_s \tag{3.7}$$

Where μ_π, μ_c and μ_s represent noise variables for inflation, country and real exchange rate risks respectively.

Depositors' utility function can be described as

$$U^D = E(r^{portfolio}) - c_D Var(r^{portfolio})/2 \tag{3.8}$$

Where $r^{portfolio}$ is the average real return of the deposit portfolio, c_D is a constant that shows aversion to risk and takes a value above zero, and Var is the variance operator.

8 Economists take note however, that this condition is limited to the extent by which prices and wages are denominated in foreign currency and as "measured by the pass-through coefficient of exchange rate changes in prices being moderate" (p. 327).

If the share of foreign deposits in the portfolio is $\lambda^{foreign}$ and the share of cross border deposits is γ^{cross}, then

$$\lambda^{foreign} = \lambda^{*} - \frac{\delta_D^I}{c_D V} \tag{3.9}$$

$$\gamma^{cross} = 1 - \delta^{x} / (c_D S_{cc}) \tag{3.10}$$

Where δ_D^I and δ^x represent the expected local and foreign deposit rate differences on foreign currency. V represents the variance of real returns between local currency and foreign currency; S_{cc} is variance-covariance matrix and equals zero. The variables used in Eqs. (3.9) and (3.10) are defined as:

$$V = Var(r^{local} - r^{foreign}) = S_{\pi\pi} + S_{ss} + 2S_{\pi s} \tag{3.11}$$

$$\delta_D^I = E(r^{local} - r^{foreign}) \tag{3.12}$$

$$\delta^X = E(r^{foreign} - r^{Cross}) \tag{3.13}$$

From Eq. (3.9), we can solve for λ^* (the share of foreign currency deposits in the optimal investment portfolio), and obtain:

$$\lambda^{*} = \frac{(S_{\pi\pi} + S_{\pi s})}{(S_{\pi\pi} + S_{ss} + 2S_{\pi s})} = \frac{Var(\pi)}{Cov(\pi, e)} \tag{3.14}$$

Where "e" denotes the nominal rate of devaluation. According to this model, the optimum amount of foreign currency deposits in the investor's portfolio depends on inflation and foreign exchange risk.

A. Ize and E. Levy-Yeyati are among the first that provided evidence for this relationship (Ize and Levy-Yeyati, 2003). The authors compared actual and MVP dollarization ratios for a sample of 46 dollarized economies. Their study revealed two important findings:

1. The optimum level of foreign currency deposits that minimizes variance in a portfolio consisting of local and foreign currency deposits determines the actual dollarization ratio in an economy. The coefficient of the MVP level (λ^*) of foreign currency deposits ranges from 0.761 to 0.794 and is highly significant with a 1% significance level in all three specifications of their panel estimations, based on 46 countries.
2. When the share of foreign currency deposits at the MVP level is entered into the same equation with the inflation rate in the economy, it reduces the explanatory power of the inflation rate. This means that risk, measured as the volatility of inflation and the real exchange rate, is a better indicator of dollarization in an economy than inflation rates.

3.5.2.2 Evidence that Supports the MVP Theory

The MVP theory is supported by a growing body of evidence. De Nicolo, Honohan and Ize (2005) tested the MVP theory by running regressions on the determinants of dollarization. The authors use MVP portfolio coefficients as determinants of dollarization and use other variables such as inflation, institutional variables, inflation targeting dummy and transition economy dummy. In 12 different OLS specifications on the causes of dollarization, the MVP coefficient is significant in all but one. According to their findings, a 2% increase in the share of the foreign currency component of the MVP raises the dollarization ratio in the economy by 1%.

In a more recent study, Neanidis and Savva (2009) tested the validity of the MVP theory on an unbalanced panel dataset of monthly observations for 11 transition economies (Armenia, Bulgaria, Czech Republic, Estonia, Georgia, Kyrgyz Republic, Latvia, Poland, Romania, Russia, and Ukraine) for the period between 1993 to 2006.

The authors define MVP in their analysis as $mvp = \sigma^2_{vt} / cov_{vut}$ where the numerator stands for the conditional variance of inflation and the denominator represents the conditional covariance between inflation and depreciation of the nominal exchange rate. For the short-term dollarization measure, the authors utilize differences in the monthly loan and deposit dollarization ratios. By doing so, they evaluate the determinants of not only the deposit dollarization but also loan dollarization.

The authors divide the countries in their sample as low, medium and high dollarization and announce their results accordingly. The authors use the following as regressors: the exchange rate factor, money base factor and an error-correction term; changes in banks' net foreign assets and some commonly used control variables such as interest rate differentials; the share of dollarization in the minimum variance portfolio; the change in the rate of inflation; an index of asymmetry of exchange rate movements and an index of exchange rate intervention. For the long term analysis, the authors utilize 6 different specifications and utilize a battery of econometric models, including the OLS, fixed effects, random effects, AR and Feasible Generalized Least Squares (FGLS).[9,10]

---

9 The authors use FGLS estimator for their robustness tests with panel heteroscedasticity and panel specific autocorrelation with AR(1) disturbances.

10 Feasible Generalized Least Squares (FGLS) is developed in two stages. In the first stage, the model is estimated by any model that provides consistent estimators (like the OLS model). The residuals from this model are used to build a consistent estimator of the errors covariance matrix by adding additional constraints to better describe this process. These control variables can include time series regressors as well as some other theoretical assumptions to ensure that a consistent estimator is estimated. In the second stage, the consistent estimator of the covariance matrix of the errors is used under the Generalized Least Squares model (GLS).

As a note of caution, it is important to bear in mind that even though the GLS is more efficient than OLS under heteroscedasticity or autocorrelation, this is not true for the Feasible Generalized Least Squares model. Provided the errors variance—covariance matrix is consistently estimated; the estimator is asymptotically more efficient. However, for a small sample size, the FGLS can be actually less efficient than OLS. (Baltagi, 2008)

The authors find that in the short run, a depreciation of the local currency induces depositors to switch the currency composition of their deposits toward a heavier weighting of foreign currencies, while a monetary expansion of the local currency promotes local-currency deposits. The results also offer support to the negative impact of the deposits interest rate differential on short-run deposit dollarization. This means that as the local currency interest rates rise, incentives to keep savings in foreign currency decline. The findings suggest that the share of foreign currency deposits in the minimum variance portfolio affects the level of deposit dollarization. However, this effect is visible only in the long run. The estimations for the short-term determinants of deposit dollarization yield insignificant results for the MVP variable. The authors explain this outcome as a result of agents' ability to better assess the differences associated with the volatility of inflation versus that of depreciation in the long run. The researchers also fail to find any significant link between deposit dollarization and inflation in the short run.

Court, Ozsoz and Rengifo (2012) provide another study that empirically evaluates the minimum variance portfolio argument as an instrument of assessing the impact of deposit dollarization on financial deepening. In defining their MVP variable, the authors follow the recent work of Neanidis and Savva (2009) who estimate the MVP as the ratio of the conditional variance of inflation to the conditional covariance between inflation and depreciation of the nominal exchange rate. By using dollarization data from 40 countries, the authors show that deposit dollarization has a negative impact on financial depth of a country when the MVP ratio of foreign currency deposits is used as an instrument.

3.5.3 Institutions Argument

A new and noteworthy perspective on the causes of dollarization is the so-called "Institutional View". The basic hypothesis of this theory is that economic agents place more trust in higher quality institutions, and will have faith in the efforts the government takes to control inflation if financial and governmental institutions are robust. If agents believe in these policies and observe that there are strong institutions that can support this government effort, they can then reduce their dollar holdings.

The Heritage Foundation's index of economic freedom is one of the most well-known indices that measures the credibility of institutions. The index consists of 10 indicators: Property Rights, Freedom from Corruption, Fiscal Freedom, Government Spending, Business Freedom, Labor Freedom, Monetary freedom, Trade freedom, Investment freedom and financial Freedom. For more information, we refer the reader to the Heritage Foundation webpage.[11]

11 http://www.heritage.org/

First mentioned by Eduardo Levy-Yeyati in his 2006 article in Economic Policy, this perspective sees the emergence of dollarization in an economy as an outcome of "the collateral cost of low institutional credibility." In this paper, Levy-Yeyati tests the institutional view argument by using a composite index of six institutional quality measures that includes ordinal measures such as the rule of law and corruption in an economy and Country Policy and Institutional Assessment (CPIA) variables assembled by the World Bank. By using dollarization ratios at the end of 1999 as the dependent variable, the author estimates the impact of institutional variables and other determinants (including the previous period dollarization ratio, inflation, and minimum variance portfolio) on dollarization. The coefficient of the two institutional strength variables that the author employs takes on negative and significant coefficients in his estimations, indicating that low institutional quality fosters dollarization in an economy. However, when estimated combined with per capita income, both variables become insignificant. The author argues that this may be because per capita income implicitly captures the beneficial effects of institutional strength. However, the study uses very few observations (81 in one specification and 68 in the other) and only employs OLS regression to test his model.

Other research that relates dollarization, institutions and banks' credibility has also shown that the quality and credibility of institutions is important in keeping dollarization under control. In a panel study of 34 dollarized economies, Kutan, Rengifo and Ozsoz (2012) demonstrated that institutional quality greatly improves the banking sector's profitability in a dollarized economy. The magnitude of the coefficient of this variable is significantly large; the impact of institutional quality on a bank's profitability is much greater than the impact of other variables, such as economic growth and deposit dollarization.

This evidence suggests that weak institutions depress the profitability of banks in dollarized economies. An important finding in this paper is that the coefficients of the institution variable more than offset the negative impact of dollarization on banks' profitability. Once more, this result implies that institutional quality (which encompasses Government Efficiency, Political Stability, Regulatory Quality, Rule of Law, Voice, and Corruption in the paper) is fundamental for banks' profitability. In essence, countries with strong institutions reduce banks' screening and monitoring costs, which makes the estimation of the discount rates used for project evaluation easier and allows financing of good investment projects that foster growth (and lead to further financial deepening).

Interest rates in countries with weak institutions include an institutional premium to cover banks against institutional risks. Institutions protect creditors' rights and, as shown by Galindo and Micco (2005), Djankov, McLiesh and Shleifer (2005), Dehesa, Druck and Plekhanov (2007), financial deepening and development can be explained to a great extent by the protection of creditors.

Court, Ozsoz and Rengifo (2012) present findings which show that institutional quality greatly enhances the depth of the financial system in dollarized economies.

Table 3.1: Index of economic freedom South America (2001–2015).

Year	Argentina	Bolivia	Brazil	Chile	Colombia	Paraguay	Peru	Uruguay	Venezuela
2001	68.6	68	61.9	75.1	65.6	60.3	69.6	70.7	54.6
2002	65.7	65.1	61.5	77.8	64.2	59.6	64.8	68.7	54.7
2003	56.3	64.3	63.4	76	64.2	58.2	64.6	69.8	54.8
2004	53.9	64.5	62	76.9	61.2	56.7	64.7	66.7	46.7
2005	51.7	58.4	61.7	77.8	59.6	53.4	61.3	66.9	45.2
2006	53.4	57.8	60.9	78	60.4	55.6	60.5	65.3	44.6
2007	54	54.2	56.2	77.7	59.9	58.3	62.7	68.4	47.9
2008	54.2	53.1	56.2	78.6	62.2	60	63.8	67.9	44.7
2009	52.3	53.6	56.7	78.3	62.3	61	64.6	69.1	39.9
2010	51.2	49.4	55.6	77.2	65.5	61.3	67.6	69.8	37.1
2011	51.7	50	56.3	77.4	68	62.3	68.6	70	37.6
2012	48	50.2	57.9	78.3	68	61.8	68.7	69.9	38.1
2013	46.7	47.9	57.7	79	69.6	61.1	68.2	69.7	36.1
2014	44.6	48.4	56.9	78.7	70.7	62	67.4	69.3	36.3
2015	44.1	46.8	56.6	78.5	71.7	61.1	67.7	68.6	34.3

This table presents the index of economic freedom for South American countries. The time spans from 2001 to 2015.
Source: Heritage Foundation.

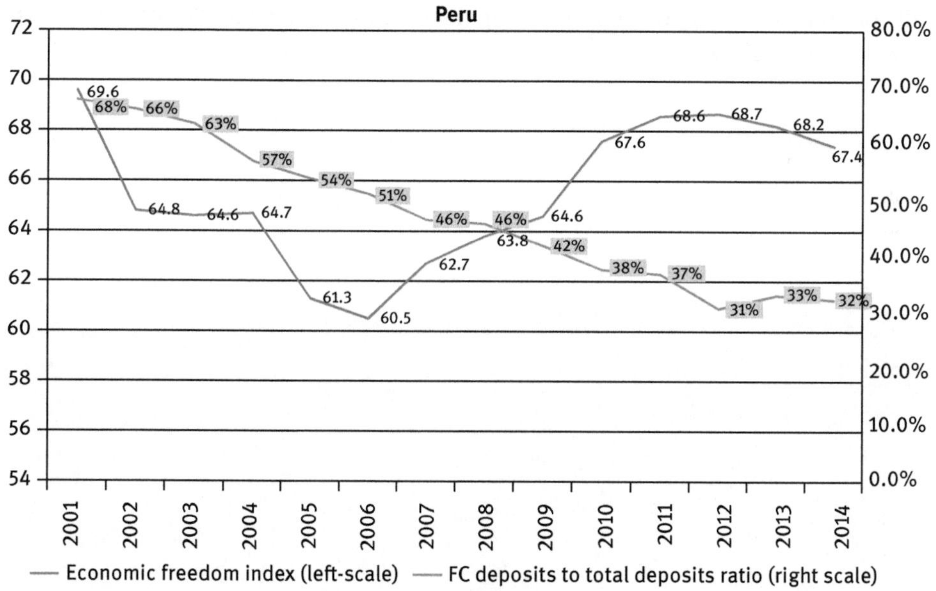

Figure 3.8: Economic freedom index vs. dollarization.
Figure 3.8 shows the deposit dollarization rates in Peru (measured as the ratio of foreign currency deposits to total deposits) versus the economic freedom index.
Sources: Central Bank of Peru, Heritage Foundation.

In a panel study of forty-four dollarized economies, the authors showed that the ratio of private credit to GDP increases as the country's institutional quality improves. This finding is robust and highly significant in more than one model.

According to these results, weak institutions, which are usually commonplace in economies that suffer from high inflation and dollarization rates, also contribute to the shallowness of financial systems. The lack of institutional quality in an economy may increase the time and effort required for banks to screen of loan applications, thus contributing to credit rationing.

It is important to note that faith in institutions is built slowly over an extended period of time. This observation can also explain why high dollarization stays high even though inflation rates are low, as economic agents are hesitant to trust the institutions that allowed the conditions for dollarization to occur. Table 3.1 presents the overall Heritage Foundation index of economic freedom for several South American countries (Argentina, Bolivia, Brazil, Chile, Colombia, Paraguay, Peru, Uruguay and Venezuela).

From Figure 3.8, one can observe a positive relationship between these two variables until approximately 2006. Subsequently, the Peruvian Economic freedom index increased from 60.5 to a maximum of 68.7 around 2012; meanwhile, the dollarization numbers continued decreasing until 2012 and stabilized at around 32% thereafter. It is clear that in Peru, institutions played an important role, although their efforts were supported by rapid macroeconomic growth and inflation stability. Institutions will continue to play a pivotal role during the coming years when Peru's spectacular growth starts to slow.

4 The Impact of Dollarization on Banking Systems

4.1 Introduction

In partially dollarized economies, the impact of dollarization on the banking industry is of particular interest to economists and academics, and receives special attention in literature.

The reason for such interest begins with the very nature of the phenomenon. In an economy where more than one currency is used, the banking system and other economic agents adapt to incorporate the adopted currency as a means of payment or unit of account alongside the local currency.

In dollarized economies it is not unusual for locals to open bank accounts in foreign as well as in local currencies. Even ATMs in such economies are designed to accept and dispense foreign currency as well as the local currency.[1]

Furthermore, in these economies, borrowing in a foreign currency is not only limited to importers. The array of foreign currency denominated loans provided by banks is wide. Agents can obtain foreign denominated loans to finance their homes (mortgages) or even to fund basic consumption purchases.

Lending in foreign currency adds additional stress on the banking system. Sharp changes in the exchange rate caused by sudden devaluations can create hardships for borrowers, as was explained in detail in Chapter 3.

To prevent an increase in loan default rates, the central banks of dollarized economies with high levels of foreign currency denominated lending act vigilantly to ensure the stability of the market. To this end, central banks intervene in foreign currency markets as necessary to prevent volatility in the exchange rate; however, the success of any intervention depends on the credibility of the central bank, the depth of foreign currency reserves and the liquidity of country's foreign exchange markets.[2] In this chapter, we describe the research that covers the crucial aspects of the impact of dollarization on local banking systems. In what follows, we try to shed light on the following questions:

i. The widespread integration of foreign currency borrowing and saving in the economy's banking system raises some questions: Why do governments in these economies allow foreign currency saving accounts and loans? Are there mechanisms used by governments to restrict these foreign denominated transactions?

1 Some ATMs in Turkey, for instance, can dispense and accept foreign currency bills for their clients. This is also a common feature of ATMs around South America (Colombia, Ecuador, and Peru, for example).

2 Also depends on their access to derivative markets that allow banks and governments to hedge their position, transferring part of their exchange risks to the global community. For more on this, read Keefe and Rengifo (2015).

ii. How do banks hedge their foreign currency liabilities (balance sheet mismatch)?
iii. What are the impacts of dollarization on banking systems in these economies?
iv. What impact does dollarization have upon monetary policy decisions?
v. What is the effect of loan dollarization by economic agents?
vi. What is the impact of dollarization on different foreign investments (Foreign Direct Investments and Portfolio Investments)?

Additionally, we examine reasons why governments in these economies have favored foreign currency accounts, evaluate the risk exposure of the banking system, outline the hedging mechanisms used by banks and discuss empirical evidence regarding the impact of dollarization on the performance of these banking systems.

We also describe how central banks react to the impact of dollarization and examine the possible impact of dollarization on households' and corporations' debt dollarization, fundamentally in an economy that faces devaluation pressures. The latter topic is of utmost interest for developing countries, mainly during periods of low economic growth and increases in foreign interest rates; this is particularly salient in light of the recent rise in US interest rates and further rises that the US FED has planned for 2016/17.

This chapter is organized as follows: In the next section, we discuss possible reasons why governments allow foreign currency denominated accounts; in Section 4.3 we highlight possible risks to the banking systems in dollarized economies, and in Section 4.4, we provide empirical evidence of the risks discussed in Section 4.3.

4.2 Why Do Governments Allow Foreign Currency Accounts and Foreign Currency Lending in the Banking System?

Recent research (such as De Nicolo, Honohan and Ize, 2005; Kutan, Ozsoz and Rengifo, 2012) has shown that banking systems are usually more fragile in dollarized economies where agents can save and borrow in foreign currency. In their study, De Nicolo, Honohan and Ize (2005) tackle the question of the extent to which dollarization is a source of banking risk. Using a large sample that includes more than one hundred economies, the authors run cross-country regressions of banks' exposure to solvency and liquidity risk arising from dollarization.[3] Their results illustrate that there is a strong negative relationship between the volatility of banks' return-on-asset ratios (ROAs) and the degree of dollarization; they also find strong evidence that as dollarization of deposits increases, so does the volatility of deposits in the banking system. Both results point to higher volatility and increased risk in the banking system in dollarized economies.

---

3 A more detailed analysis of their study will be discussed in the following subsections.

In a more recent empirical study, Kutan, Ozsoz and Rengifo (2012) looked at how financial dollarization impacted the profitability of banks in dollarized economies. The authors used the ratio of foreign currency deposits in the system versus the overall money supply in the economy, as well as several macroeconomic (changes in GDP and inflation), financial (the interest rate spread, and the ratio of loan-loss-provisions to loans and the ratio of equity to total asset-proxies for credit and capital risk) and institutional variables (government efficiency, political stability, regulatory quality, rule of law, voice and quality). This data is collected from 36 dollarized countries.

Their study showed that interest rate spreads and GDP growth rate have a positive effect on bank profitability, while dollarization of deposits exerts a negative and statistically significant impact with a one-period lag. The authors provide two possible explanations for the time lag; "First, bank managers in dollarized economies consider the previous period's dollarization ratios in determining current period holdings of cash and other assets, i.e. liquidity and asset management. Second, there is a transfer from exchange risk into default risk in dollarized banking systems i.e. as banks increase their lending in foreign currency to compensate for increases in foreign currency deposits, they increase credit default risk." (p. 479). Given such evidence, we are faced with a quandary regarding why regulators would enable banks to accept dollar deposits and lend in foreign currencies, given the apparent risks to the financial system.

There is no simple explanation for this situation. Several authors have mentioned that in times of inflation crisis, when economic agents are trying to hedge their positions to keep the value of their assets, several governments have allowed and at times encouraged deposit dollarization as a means to reduce capital flight. Dollar-denominated deposits provide liquidity buffers for banks[4] that can be used to finance businesses and contribute toward economic recovery.

Another feasible explanation as to why governments allow foreign currency accounts is that they are unable to prevent economic agents from using foreign currencies. While the authorities may not explicitly encourage the use of foreign currency accounts, there is not enough incentive for economic agents to use the local currency for everyday transactions.

From Chapter 3, we can recall that the causes of dollarization are rooted in inflation volatility (relative volatilities of returns in local and foreign currency as explained by the MPV theory) and institutional weaknesses. Therefore, governments may not easily alter the attitudes of their population in terms of foreign currency usage. Once

4 Delechat et al. (2012) find evidence in the Central American case that shows a robust positive impact of the degree of deposit dollarization on the size of liquidity buffers within the banking system. The authors see this phenomenon however as a hindrance to development of financial markets and to the transmission of monetary policy. The adverse impact of dollarization on the monetary transmission mechanism has also been investigated and proven by others such as Cas, Carrión-Menéndez and Frantischek (2011).

economic agents think the government lacks institutional credibility, the process to recover credibility can take several years, yet governments are not always completely successful in convincing their economic agents to change their behavior (see Section 3.3 in Chapter 3).

It is clear that deposit and liability dollarization imposes serious dangers to the local banking system, and these potential risks are well known to regulators in these economies.

In fact, regulatory changes in some of these economies following the 2008–2009 global financial crisis and the subsequent turbulence in global currency markets is evidence that regulators consider dollarization, especially on the liability side, as a threat to the stability of their financial systems. For example, following the steep rise in the value of the US dollar versus their local currencies, regulators in Turkey, Ukraine, Croatia, Kazakhstan and Romania[5] limited foreign currency lending by their banks between 2008 and 2010. Such policy moves are evidence that central bankers in these economies were worried about the level of exposure to foreign currency lending in their economies.

4.3 Banking Risks in a Partially Dollarized Economy

The dollarization of bank deposits and the subsequent dollarization of bank loans create risks for financial institutions that regulators need to carefully handle.

From a bank's perspective, some of their risks are currency mismatch risk (also known as balance sheet mismatch risk), exchange rate risk and default risk. From a regulator's perspective, the most apparent risk is a systemic instability risk that can have severe adverse socio-political consequences. We will look at each one of these risks in the following section.

4.3.1 Currency Mismatch Risk

In general, financial institutions operating in economies where foreign currency accounts are allowed hold deposits and liabilities in more than one currency.

In some instances, the total value of their foreign currency deposits may rival or exceed those in local currency. For instance, as of 2014 year-end the total amount of foreign currency deposits held by depository institutions in Turkey was 63% of the amount of deposits in Turkish liras.[6] As of 2010, the foreign currency liabilities held

---

5 Croatia, Kazakhstan and Romania implemented stronger provisioning requirements for foreign currency lending (Brown and Haas, 2010). Regulators in Ukraine and Turkey completely banned FC lending to households in 2008 and 2009, respectively (Ozsoz, Rengifo and Kutan, 2015).

6 Source: Turkish Bank Association.

by depository institutions in Latvia was more than 7 times those of local currency liabilities.[7]

Additionally, banks in dollarized economies have to offer their depositors interest on their foreign currency accounts. In some cases, the interest rates on these accounts may be much higher than the rates paid by depository institutions in the home country of the foreign currency. For instance, the average interest rate paid on foreign currency accounts in Azerbaijan, as of 2014, was over 8%; meanwhile the interest rates on 12-month Certificates of Deposits in the US (for denominations less than 100,000) was 0.21% in 2014 (Source: US Federal Reserve Bank). In Europe, the average interest rate paid on Euro deposits with less than one year maturity was around 0.9% as of December 2014 (Source: ECB MFI interest rate statistics, European Central Bank). See Table 4.1.

In this environment, a mismatch between assets and liabilities may occur on a bank's balance sheet if the total value of foreign currency holdings on one side of its balance sheet (whether liabilities or assets) is not equal to the other side of its balance sheet.

In most cases, the amount of foreign currency liabilities of financial institutions in partially dollarized economies exceeds foreign currency denominated assets. Obviously, banks in these economies plan for such mismatches. One solution to the problem is to use forward contracts and hedge the resulting foreign exchange risk. However, there are problems with using forward contracts; as Honig (2009) pointed out, "if a forward contract is made with other domestic banks or firms who earn revenue in [local currency] the country's aggregate net foreign exposure remains unchanged." In other words, foreign exchange risk becomes a local counterparty risk. It has not been established whether redistributing risk in such a fashion has a stabilizing effect upon that economy (Eichengreen and Hausmann, 1999).

Additionally, the derivative markets where these contracts are bought and sold may not be very liquid. Foreign banks may not be willing to write forward contracts to exchange for local currency (Eichengreen and Hausmann, 1999), or even if such contracts are available, they may not be cheap. This may limit hedging options for local banks.

The most natural way to hedge under these circumstances is to offer loans in foreign currency. A bank may recycle its foreign currency deposits simply by opening credit lines to businesses or households in the respective foreign currency. Additionally, banks earn an intermediation spread, since loans in a foreign currency will have higher interest rates compared to those paid on foreign currency deposits.

Although this may seem like an intelligent decision on bank's behalf and may reduce currency mismatch risk, such a policy may lead to other risks for banks in particular and for the economy in general. As argued by Chang and Velasco (2001),

7 Source: IMF-IFS.

Table 4.1: Average interest rates paid on foreign currency accounts (as of 2014).

Average interest rates on foreign currency deposits (as of 2014)	Percent per annum
Azerbaijan, Republic of	8.60
Tajikistan	7.43
Ukraine	6.72
Georgia	4.83
Moldova	4.17
Honduras	4.08
El Salvador	3.78
Suriname	3.30
Maldives	3.23
Anguilla	2.66
Kenya	2.58
Antigua and Barbuda	2.56
Indonesia	2.20
Eastern Caribbean Currency Union (ECCU)	1.73
Paraguay	1.63
Serbia, Republic of	1.59
Trinidad and Tobago	1.50
Oman	1.37
Dominican Republic	1.36
Macedonia, FYR	1.36
Nicaragua	1.24
St. Vincent and the Grenadines	1.15
St. Lucia	1.11
Botswana	1.07
St. Kitts and Nevis	1.03
Haiti	0.90
Argentina	0.87
Montserrat	0.86
Philippines	0.72
Grenada	0.64
Dominica	0.52
Peru	0.36
Chile	0.35
Poland	0.27
Uruguay	0.24
Bolivia	0.23

Source: IMF-IFS. Available at http://data.imf.org/.

dollarization of liabilities implies that devaluations have damaging effects on banks' balance sheets since borrowers, who in general earn in local currency, start defaulting on their obligations (credit risk). In the event of large and sudden drops in the value of the local currency (depreciations of local currency), borrowers' ability to pay may be substantially distressed. For example, bank failures were common occurrences in

East Asian economies during the Asian Financial Crisis following the devaluation of local currencies.

Dollarization and currency mismatches on banks' balance sheets have proven to be highly correlated with episodes of financial crises in developing countries. The Asian Financial Crisis and the 2001 Argentinian Debt Crisis provide a useful example of the correlation between currency mismatches and banks' balance sheets (see Figure 4.1). Until the onset of the crisis in 2001, the total value of local currency deposits in Argentina was less than the value of foreign currency deposits in the banking system. This meant that there were more foreign currency denominated deposits in Argentinian banks' than local currency deposits. This spread continued to widen at an annual rate of 71% until 2001. Following the crisis, the forced conversion of foreign currency deposits into pesos reversed the trend.

4.3.2 From Currency Mismatch Risk to Default Risk

Financial institutions in dollarized economies have various tools available for hedging against exchange rate risks. Financial derivatives, such as foreign currency swaps or options, can be utilized to protect the institution from sudden exchange

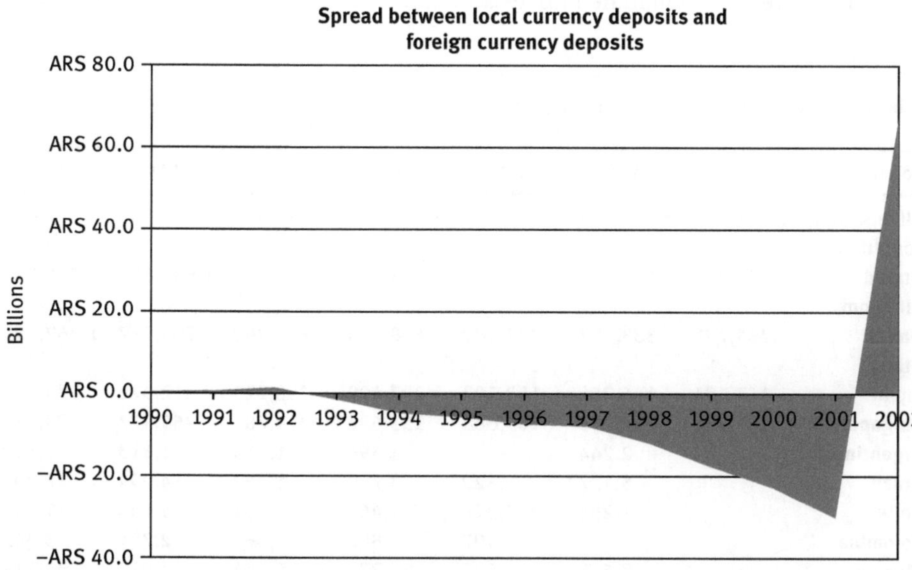

Figure 4.1: Spread between local currency deposits and foreign currency deposits—Argentina. Figure 4.1 shows the spread between local currency deposits in the Argentinian banking system to the level of foreign currency deposits in terms of billions of pesos.
Source: Yeyati (2006).

rate movements. However, the derivative markets in several of the dollarized economies are not as developed as their developed counterparts. This limits the ability of financial institutions to use market instruments to hedge their positions. If hedging strategies are available in less developed economies, the costs of hedging are usually higher, perhaps to the point of being prohibitive. The next table presents the OTC foreign exchange derivatives turnover for the largest markets (England, USA, Japan and Singapore) and for several Latin American countries (Argentina, Brazil, Chile, Colombia, Mexico and Peru). From Table 4.2 one can appreciate the significant difference in derivatives availability for these Latin American countries.

Given the environment described previously, most financial institutions opt to make loans in foreign currencies, thereby creating foreign currency denominated assets to counter foreign currency liabilities. However, attempts to cancel mismatch risk can merely transform the risk into default risk, which is potentially more dangerous not only to the stability of the banking system, but also for the economy in general. The hypothesized connection is illustrated in Figure 4.2.

As argued by De Nicolo, Honohan and Ize (2005), the degree of currency mismatch intensifies if local prices and wages are set in local currency while financial assets are held in foreign currency. In an environment where borrowers' ability to repay their loans are not indexed to foreign currency, exchange rate risk translates itself into default risk. At the time of sudden and/or permanent exchange rate increases (depreciations), borrowers who earn in local currency face difficulties covering their foreign denominated losses and naturally have potentially higher default

Table 4.2: OTC foreign exchange derivatives turnover.

Country	1995	1998	2001	2004	2007	2010	2013
All reporting countries	1,632,749	2,099,322	1,704,681	2,608,106	4,281,096	5,043,038	6,671,446
United Kingdom	478,832	685,157	541,699	835,279	1,483,210	1,853,594	2,725,993
United States	265,799	383,357	272,582	498,644	745,202	904,357	1,262,799
Japan	167,681	146,268	152,702	207,409	250,223	312,326	374,215
Singapore	107,256	144,936	103,684	133,636	241,785	265,977	383,075
Argentina		2,244	–	696	1,113	1,613	1,360
Brazil		5,127	5,529	3,790	5,762	14,094	17,203
Chile		1,255	2,328	2,462	4,003	5,544	11,956
Colombia			397	802	1,860	2,794	3,343
Mexico		8,659	8,593	15,270	15,314	17,019	32,112
Peru			241	306	805	1,425	2,171

Table 4.2 presents the OTC foreign exchange derivatives turnover for selected countries. The frequency of observations is triennial and the numbers represent USD millions.
Source: BIS. Available at http://stats.bis.org/statx/toc/DER.html.

Mechanics of Hypothesized Connection

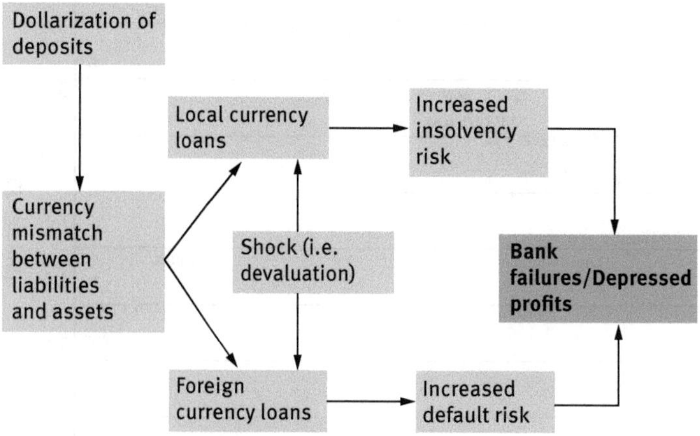

Figure 4.2: From currency mismatch risk to default risk.
This diagram presents the mechanism by which banks can be transforming their currency mismatch risk to default risk.
Source: Authors' design.

rates for foreign currency indexed loans.[8] This means that while the banks may match the right and the left side of the balance sheet in terms of currency composition, they cannot prevent currency mismatch risks completely. The risk reappears as default risk on the balance sheet, pushing banking institutions to make additional loan loss provisions, to increase reserves or to take other security measures. Banks need to take these measures voluntary or may be forced to do so by government regulation.

Figure 4.3 shows some examples of loan loss provisions (LLP) to total loan ratios for selected economies against the exchange rate (in terms of local currency per US Dollar). As illustrated, the LLP to total ratio increases when the country's currency loses value versus the USD. This can be attributed to expectations about borrowers' falling repayment rates during periods of currency depreciation (as explained previously).

8 The increase in the likelihood of defaults is something that we observe during 2014–2015. Before those years and due to developed market monetary policies including quantitative financial easing (American and European), the liquidity of USD (and other strong currencies) was high and USD interest rates were significantly lower than local currency rates. Furthermore, during those years, exchange rates in developing economies were relatively stable, giving economic agents a sense of safety concerning the real purchasing power of their incomes in local currencies. This environment motivated economic agents (households, corporations and governments) to look for and, ultimately to get, loans in dollars instead of local currencies (business or commercial loans as well as consumption loans and mortgages). The most pernicious and dangerous effects are still forthcoming, since agents' savings are most likely being used to help avoid defaults. However, as the current global macroeconomic environment appears to be the norm and not a short term event, agents, the banking systems and economies will be facing strong pressures that need to be addressed in order to avoid systemic socio-economic problems.

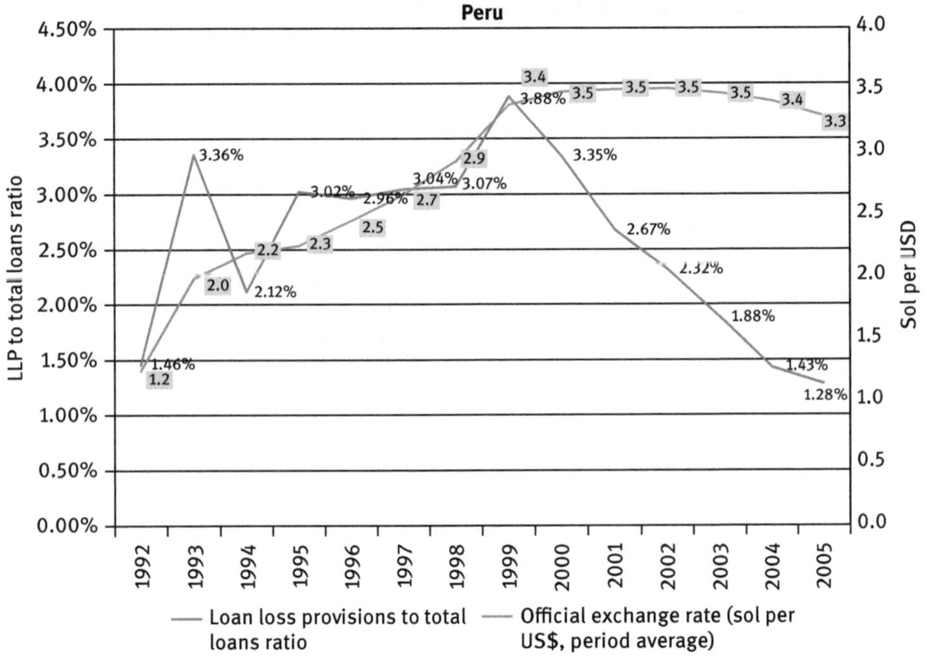

Figure 4.3: Loan loss provisions to total loans ratio versus the exchange rate—Peru.
This diagram presents the ratio of banks' loan loss provisions (LLP) to total loans in Peru versus the official exchange rate (Sol per USD).
Source: World Bank Databank, Bankscope Database.

Table 4.3 and Figure 4.4 show the relationship between the depreciation of local currencies in selected economies versus the ratio of nonperforming loans in the banking systems to overall loans. As can be seen from the fitted regression line, there appears to be a positive relationship between the two variables, confirming our argument. As the value of the local currency falls, the ratio of nonperforming loans to the overall loan portfolio in the banking system increases. This can be linked to the existence of foreign currency denominated loans in the banking system.

This potential problem is an incentive for banks to act conservatively when selecting borrowers, potentially decreasing the funds available to the economy. This conjecture has been proven in recent studies. Court, Rengifo and Ozsoz (2012) illustrated that deposit dollarization has an adverse effect on the financial depth of an economy (measured as the ratio of private credit to GDP). In other words, increases in the deposit dollarization ratio reduce the amount of credit extended by the banking system. For example, bankers in a partially dollarized economy may only consider exporters as potential clients for foreign currency denominated credit, since exporters' incomes are inversely related to the value of the local currency. For exporters, a

Table 4.3: Depreciation of the local currency vs the US dollar and the ratio of nonperforming loans to total loan portfolio in selected economies.

Country name	NPL to total loans average (%)	Depreciation versus the USD (%)	Period
Afghanistan	14.4	23.2	2010–2014
Albania	11.4	−13.4	2003–2014
Algeria	14.2	10.9	2009–2014
Angola	10.9	91.9	2002–2004
Azerbaijan	6.2	−2.4	2009–2014
Bosnia and Herzegovina	10.1	−30.6	2000–2014
Brazil	4.6	118.3	1997–2014
Bulgaria	10.5	−12.3	1997–2014
Burundi	9.1	25.7	2010–2014
Colombia	5.5	75.4	1997–2014
Comoros	1.5	−0.2	2010–2014
Costa Rica	2.1	109.3	1998–2014
Gabon	9.1	−30.6	2000–2014
Jordan	9.9	0.1	1998–2014
Kazakhstan	11.7	16.9	2002–2014
Lebanon	8.4	−0.6	1998–2014
Malaysia	8.8	16.3	1997–2014
Mexico	4.2	67.9	1997–2014
Montenegro	11.5	−6.4	2004–2014
Namibia	2.4	26.1	2001–2014
Paraguay	7.0	63.7	1998–2014
Peru	5.9	6.6	1997–2014
Romania	17.4	367.2	1997–2014
Rwanda	23.5	53.9	2001–2014
Serbia	17.7	37.3	2002–2014
Sierra Leone	20.7	116.2	2000–2014
South Africa	3.5	96.3	1998–2014
Tanzania	11.8	17.4	2010–2014
Thailand	11.9	−21.5	1998–2014
Uganda	5.6	109.6	1998–2014

Source: World Bank Databank.

depreciation of local currency is beneficial for their business since their global competitiveness improves (their products are perceived as being cheaper). However, in most of these dollarized economies, the level of foreign currency deposits is so high that it is not possible to offset the foreign currency liabilities on the balance sheet by only lending to export-related industries. Consequently, banks end up lending to many other borrowers, whose incomes may be positively correlated with the value of the local currency.

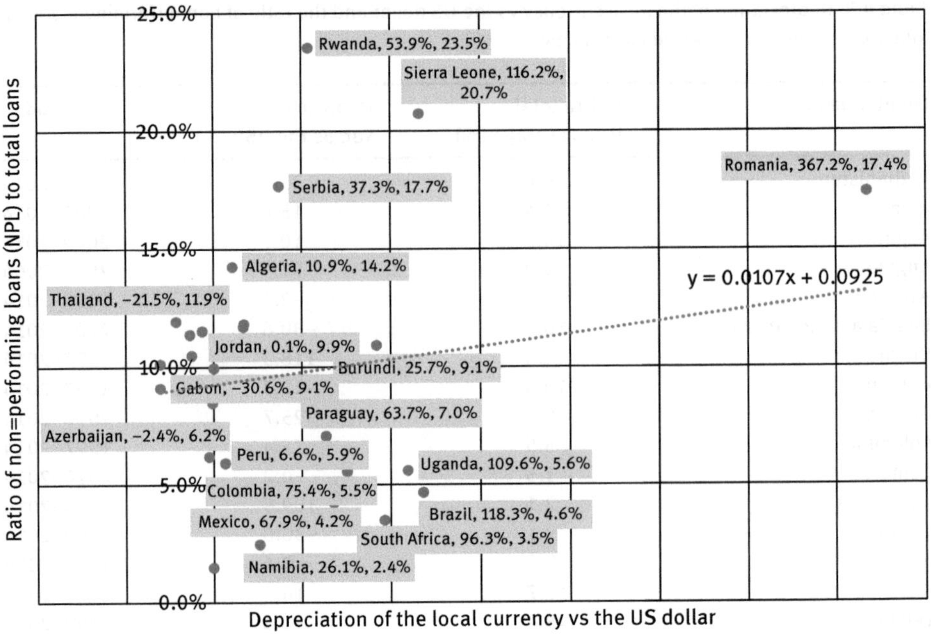

Figure 4.4: Depreciation of local currency vs the US dollar and nonperforming loans ratio in selected economies.
Source: World Bank Databank.

The dollarization mismatch issue has also a direct impact on fiscal policy. In general, we can observe that governments levy taxes in the local currency, but borrow in foreign currencies to limit short-run debt-servicing costs or to signal a commitment to a stable exchange rate (De Nicolo, Honohan and Ize, 2005).

As we have clearly seen, currency mismatches can have detrimental effects on the financial systems of dollarized economies through their effect on the private and public sectors. In the next section, we will evaluate the existing empirical evidence on this issue.

4.4 Empirical Evidence

Empirical evidence of the negative impact of deposit dollarization to banks' balance sheet risks is provided by the theoretical link that has been empirically tested and proven.

De Nicolo, Honohan and Ize (2005) were among the first to show that dollarization has a negative effect on solvency and could be a source of liquidity risk for banks. By using data for 1995–2000 period, the authors measure the distance-to-default for banks by using the banks' average Z-scores[9] over the period. Their results show that the ratio of non-performing loans to the total loan portfolio increases as a result of an increase in the average dollarization ratio. This means that as the dollarization of bank deposits increases, a bank's probability of default also increases along with its ratio of non-performing loans to its total loan portfolio. This relationship is robust and highly significant under different specifications.[10] However, it is important to note that these findings are limited by the low number of observations used. In the authors' estimations where distance-to-default, measured by the Z-score, is the dependent variable, the number of observations ranges from 34 to 69. The number of observations in their other estimations, where the NPL ratio is used as the dependent variable, were as few as 31.

Based on their results, the authors make a number of policy recommendations, including:

- Control inflation to promote financial development as opposed to outlawing onshore foreign currency deposit accounts.
- Follow a two-lane approach in reducing dollarization, involving discouraging the use of the dollar and enhancing the attractiveness of the local currency.
- Make a credible commitment to maintain price stability.
- Strengthen the institutional environment and commit to transparent policies.

The authors suggest monetary authorities increase the attractiveness of the local currency to discourage the use of foreign currencies as an alternative saving mechanism. Monetary authorities can follow several policies to increase the attractiveness of the local currency. In the short run, authorities could adopt an inflation targeting regime to bring down inflation which includes raising domestic interest rates. Over the long run, authorities can strengthen and improve the quality of institutions while ensuring the independence of the central bank.

More recent studies also reach similar conclusions. Kutan, Ozsoz and Rengifo (2012) compile a much larger dataset than the one used by De Nicolo, Honohan and Ize (2005). Kutan, Ozsoz and Rengifo used the level of foreign currency deposits in a country's banking system to the M2 money base as the main dollarization measure in 36 countries, obtaining over 400 data points of aggregated balance sheet information which tested the impact of deposit dollarization on the level of bank profitability.

These authors test whether the hypothesized link between currency mismatches and the increased level of default risk holds, and if the link holds, whether banks'

9 The authors compute the Z score as (K+ROA)/α where K is the equity capital-to-asset ratio and ROA is the return on assets; α represents the standard deviation of returns on assets. Z score provides information on the probability of insolvency; higher scores indicate less risk, while lower scores translate into higher probability of insolvency.

10 The authors used a stepwise estimation. The dollarization variable is always significant. The econometric techniques used include the 2SLS and several OLS models.

profitability is depressed in dollarized economies by estimating bank performance using bank profits before taxes (adjusted by the total assets as the dependent variable).

The authors used bank and industry specific variables such as credit quality, measured by the ratio of bank loan loss provisions to overall loans and bank capital ratio (measured simply as equity to total assets), as well as country specific macroeconomic variables including inflation, economic growth, average intermediation spread and the measure of institutional quality. In terms of econometric specification, the economists used not only a fixed effects model but also a dynamic GMM model to see the robustness and consistency of their results.

Their results confirm those of De Nicolo, Honohan and Ize (2005), suggesting that there is a clear inverse relationship between the level of deposit dollarization and bank performance in dollarized banking systems. Surprisingly, the authors' results suggest that the negative impact of dollarization is apparent only after a time-lag. While the findings show that current period dollarization ratios do not seem to have any significant effect on banks' overall performance in an economy, previous period dollarization ratios have a robust and significant effect on bank profitability.

The authors attribute the rationale for this outcome to bank managers' adaptive expectations, and the fact that bank managers plan for the current period usually by reflecting on previous period data. Therefore, accounting for changes in deposit dollarization ratios should have at least a one-year time lag as bank managers manage their asset and liquidity positions. Bankers determine their portfolio composition and loan loss reserves at the beginning of the year.

This result is confirmed through analyzing banks' cash holdings; bankers prefer to hold more liquid or less-risky portfolio positions in the presence of high deposit dollarization, decreasing lending and thus reducing profitability.

The negative relationship between bank profitability and deposit dollarization can be explained by the increase in default rates as a consequence of currency depreciations. Currency depreciations make banks more selective in their lending (reducing their market participation) and cause financial institutions to suffer losses due to defaults.

Another interesting finding in Kutan, Ozsoz and Rengifo (2012) is the prominent effect of institutions on banks' profitability and cash holdings. Banks in countries with strong institutions more than offset the negative impact of dollarization on their profitability and hold lower cash positions. This finding is robust in all models tested.

A further study that analyzes the impact of such a connection between profits and dollarization is provided by Court, Rengifo and Ozsoz (2012). The authors, building on the works of Kutan, Ozsoz and Rengifo (2012) and De Nicolo, Honohan and Ize (2005), investigate whether there is any effect on the depth of a financial system arising from the relationship between dollarization and bank profitability. In other words, the authors take the research question one step further and investigate whether such a relationship exists, as illustrated by Figure 4.5.

Dollarization on Financial Depth of an Economy

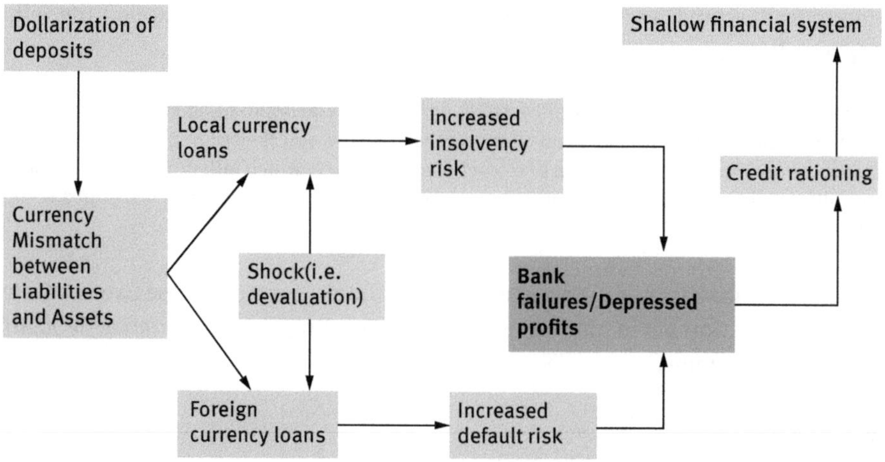

Figure 4.5: Theoretical linkage between dollarization and financial deepening.
This diagram presents the relationship between dollarization and financial deepening.
Source: Authors' sketch

Using a sample of 44 developing countries with high dollar denominated deposits and different levels of inflation, the authors study the effect of deposit dollarization (measured as the ratio dollar deposits to total bank deposits) on financial deepening of these countries (measured as the ratio of domestic credit extended by the banking system to the private sector to the GDP).

The authors analyze the results by region (Asia, Transition Economies and Latin America) and introduce the use of a different coefficient of the Minimum Variance Portfolio as suggested by Neanidis and Savva (2009).[11] They also use the specification proposed by De Nicolo, Honohan and Ize (2005). In order to make their results comparable, Court, Rengifo and Ozsoz (2012) follow the methodology of De Nicolo, Honohan and Ize (2005) and also use the same institutional, regulatory and macroeconomic variables.

As the authors initially surmised, deposit dollarization has a consistent and negative impact on financial deepening, except in high-inflation economies. For the forty-four dollarized economies included in the sample, deposit dollarization exerts a negative impact on the amount of private credit extended by the banking system to

11 The coefficient used by Neanidis and Savva (2009) is computed using the nominal inflation rate (as opposed to the real effective inflation rate).

the economy. However, when inflation is controlled for, the negative impact disappears and turns positive. This suggests that in high inflationary economies, dollarization has a moderating effect on inflation. This finding reasserts the importance of inflation in understanding the effects of dollarization. The authors explain the relationship as follows:

> While dollarization may have a positive effect on the financial depth of an economy with high inflation by providing local agents an alternative way to save and thus preventing capital flight, it seems to undermine the extension of credit in an economy in which inflation has already been controlled by increasing currency or default risks through currency mismatches. (Court et al., 2012, p. 50)

Therefore, policy makers in dollarized economies should consider these two separate effects of dollarization when instituting policies regarding foreign currency deposits in their banking systems.

5 Dollarization, Financial Deepening and Financial Inclusion

5.1 Introduction

Financial deepening refers to the availability of funds provided by financial intermediaries to final users (individuals, governments and firms). Additionally, financial inclusion refers to the availability of financial products (deposits, savings, loans, etc.), and how easily or widely these products are accessed by most economic agents in an economy.

Literature has shown that over the long run, financial deepening is an important catalyst for economic growth in emerging markets (see Darrat, Elkhal and McCallum, 2006 among others). Countries with deep credit markets enable entrepreneurs to tap into much needed capital for growth. In return, growth provides jobs and economic stability.

Figure 5.1 shows the average growth rates in 119 developing countries plotted against the average credit to GDP ratios for the 2000–2014 period. We can observe that there is a positive relationship between financial depth and the country's growth rate. The Slope coefficient of the best fit line presented in the figure is positive (0.01) but not statistically significant at 5%. The correlation is +0.12.

Figure 5.2 shows the same relationship but this time, only using data from developing countries with shallow financial systems (where credit to GDP ratio is 50% or less). The positive correlation we observed in Figure 5.1 is less clear in countries with shallow financial systems.

Figures 5.3 and 5.4, show the evolution of financial deepening in two important regions, Latin America and Transition economies.

Figures 5.5 and 5.6 show the relationship between financial deepening and growth in these two regions. While Latin American countries show a direct relationship between the two variables, for transition economies, we observe an inverse relationship between financial depth and GDP growth.

The following sections of the chapter are as follows. Section 5.2 reviews some of the existing literature on financial depth and dollarization and analyzes the empirical evidence regarding this relationship; Section 5.3 discusses an economic development issue known as financial inclusion and its relationship with dollarization, and Section 5.4 examines the role of Bitcoin as a new form of dollarization.

5.2 What We Know about Financial Depth and Dollarization: A Review

The relationship between dollarization and financial depth influences the macroeconomic stability of countries, as measured through growth rates and the volatility of

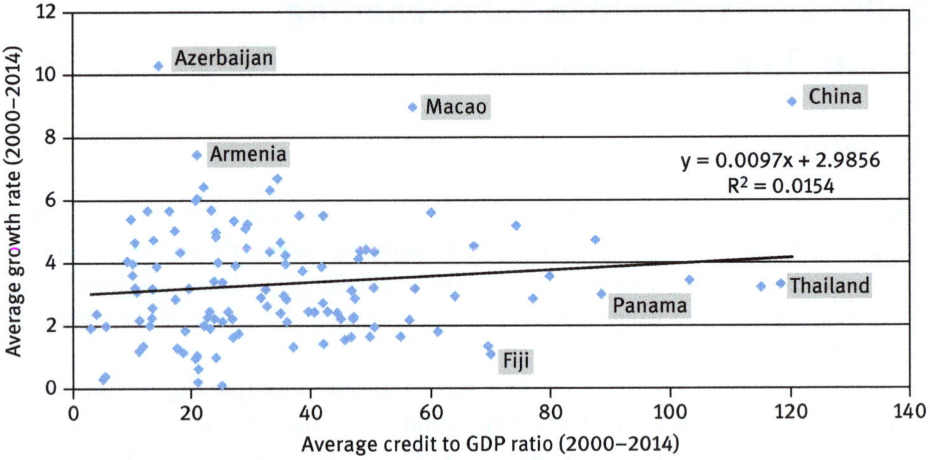

Figure 5.1: Financial depth vs growth rates (all countries).
Figure 5.1 shows the average growth rates for 119 developing countries between 2000 and 2014 plotted against average credit to GDP ratios for the same period. The equation for the best fitted linear trendline is: Average Growth Rate = 0.0097 * Average Credit to GDP Ratio + 2.98.
Source: World Bank.

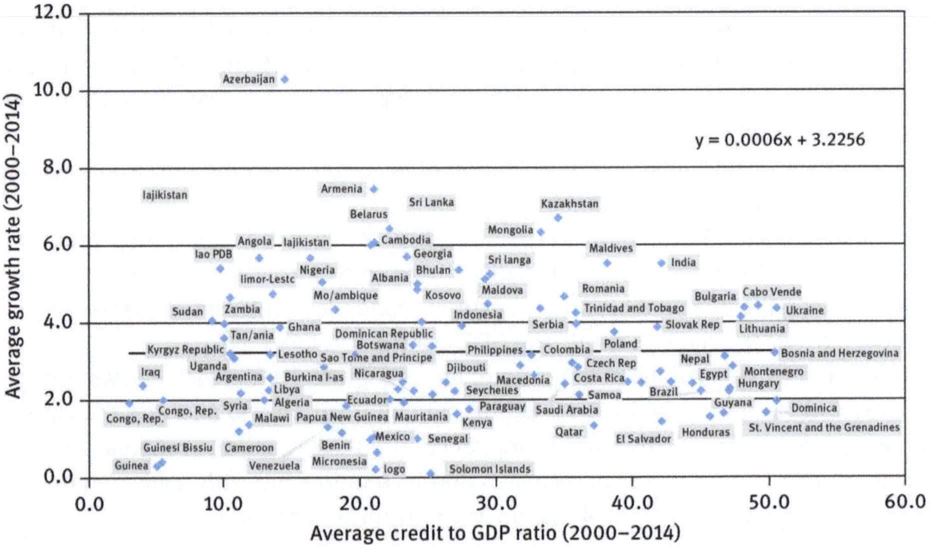

Figure 5.2: Financial depth vs growth rates (shallow financial systems).
Figure 5.2 shows the average growth rates for 100 developing countries with shallow financial systems (where credit to GDP ratio is 50% or lower) between 2000 and 2014 plotted against average credit to GDP ratios for the same period. The equation for the best fitted linear trendline is: Average Growth Rate = 0.0006 * Average Credit to GDP Ratio + 3.22.
Source: World Bank.

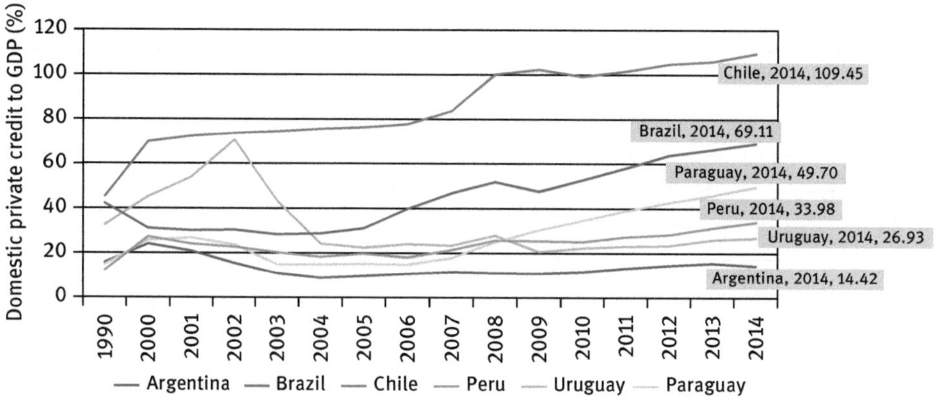

Figure 5.3. Development of financial depth in Latin American economies (2000–2014).
Figure 5.3 shows the evolution of financial depth (measured as the ratio of domestic private credit to GDP in percentages) in selected Latin American economies between 2000 and 2014.
Source: World Bank Databank.

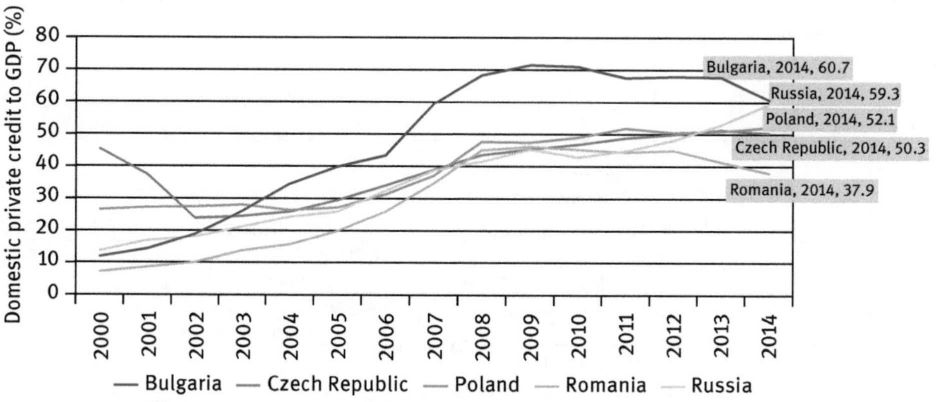

Figure 5.4: Financial deepening in selected transition economies (2000–2014).
Figure 5.4 shows the evolution of financial depth (measured as the ratio of domestic private credit to GDP in percentages) in selected transition economies between 2000 and 2014.
Source: World Bank Databank.

inflation rates. We know from empirical research that a low inflation rate is closely linked with the strengthening of financial systems, and inflation remains low as a financial system becomes increasingly deep and sophisticated. In general, in an inflationary environment, banks lend and allocate less capital, stock markets become smaller and less liquid, and savers save less, preferring physical assets to financial securities.

As we discussed in earlier chapters, one of the main reasons for the appearance of dollarization in an economy is the erosion of money's function as a store of value (the

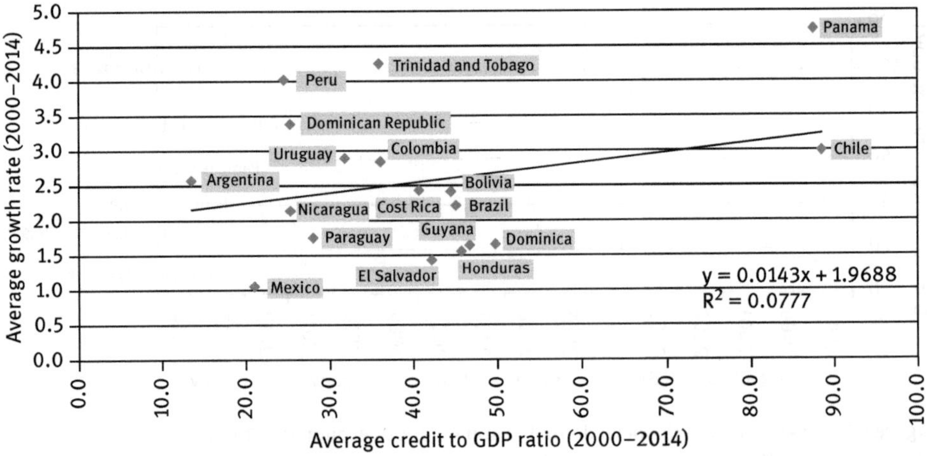

Figure 5.5: Financial deepening and economic growth (Latin American economies, 2000–2014). Figure 5.5 shows the average growth rates for 18 Latin American and Caribbean countries between 2000 and 2014 plotted against average credit to GDP ratios for the same period. The equation for the best fitted linear trendline is: Average Growth Rate = 0.0143 * Average Credit to GDP Ratio + 1.97. Source: World Bank.

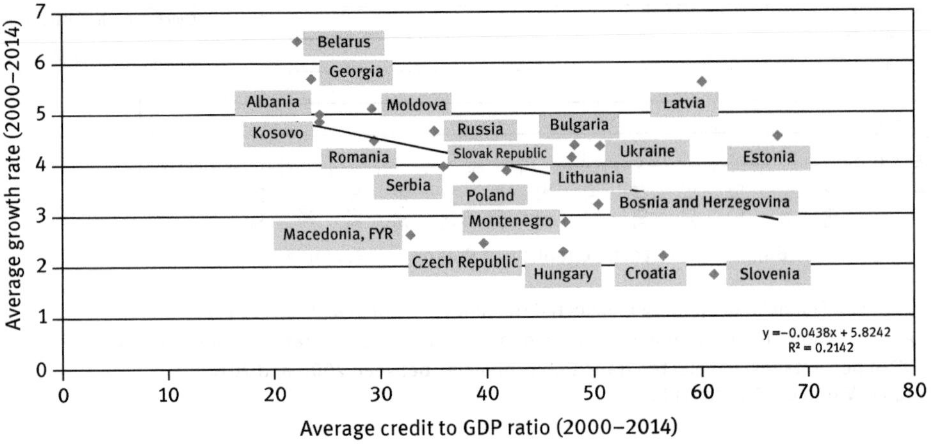

Figure 5.6: Financial deepening and economic growth (Latin American economies) (2000–2014). Figure 5.6 shows the average growth rates for 22 transition economies between 2000 and 2014 plotted against average credit to GDP ratios for the same period. The equation for the best fitted linear trendline is: Average Growth Rate = −0.044 * Average Credit to GDP Ratio + 5.82. Source: World Bank.

Currency Substitution hypothesis). High and chronic inflation rates eventually lead to high dollarization ratios. It is important to remember that under this scenario, dollarization gives consumers a shelter from domestic inflation and enables savers to retain the value of their savings. To reiterate, dollarization does not only serve as a hedging instrument but also provides an incentive for saving which is very much needed in developing financial systems. As Feige (2003) points out, by offering an alternative investment mechanism, dollarization helps prevent capital flight from those economies and, by contributing to keep savings in the local economy, may also positively contribute to financial depth despite high inflation.

Even though there have been studies on the effects of full dollarization on real economic variables such as growth and employment, there has been limited research performed to analyze the effects of partial dollarization on the development of financial systems. De Nicolo, Honohan and Ize (2005) are the first to empirically assess the effect of dollarization of bank deposits on the financial deepening of a country.

As indicated by these economists, any econometric investigation of financial deepening and dollarization is prone to endogeneity problems since "... many of the factors influential for monetary depth are also among the determinants of dollarization" (p. 1705). The authors note that the coexistence of the two phenomena could be a result of other factors, rather than having a causal relationship.

In order to deal with this endogeneity problem, the authors used an instrumental variable method which included instruments that are the causes of dollarization in their analysis. Their findings suggest that for high inflation economies, financial depth and inflation seem to be positively related. They use an interaction term between the two variables (dollarization and the logarithm of inflation) and find a significant and positive coefficient.[1] The authors test if this relationship is present in high inflation countries and their findings suggest that for higher inflation economies, dollarization does indeed strengthen the financial system through the moderating effect of dollarization on the adverse effects of inflation upon monetary depth. The authors were not able to find the same result for low inflation economies.

Based on the previous findings, they contend that "[...] dollarization may have little impact on monetary depth where risk factors summarized by inflation are low [...]" (De Nicolo, Honohan and Ize, 2005, pp. 1712). Furthermore, they recognize that the more the dollarized the system, the riskier it becomes. The authors explain that this is mainly because "... dollarized financial systems are exposed to both solvency and liquidity risk. As regards [to] solvency, the main risk results from currency mismatches in the event of large depreciations." Liquidity risk arises when depositors fear that local banks will not be able to honor the claims on their deposits. Such fears

1 In their Equation (2.2) on p. 1706, the interaction term (Dol*log(inflat)) has a positive coefficient of 0.144 and a t-stat value of 3.7 which indicated significance at the 99% level of confidence. In their equation, "Dol" represents dollarization and "log(inflat)" represents the natural logarithm of inflation rates.

may be the result of an increase in risk premiums on foreign currency deposits in local banks. This risk premium is a direct result of the fact that local banks may hold large claims against the government in these economies, and as a result of the fact that local banks may "end up on-lending domestically a large share of their dollar deposits, effectively transferring the currency risk to their unhedged clients and retaining the resulting credit risk." (pp. 1712–1713)

Court, Ozsoz and Rengifo (2012) performed a further empirical study that explored the links between dollarization and financial deepening. The authors estimated the impact of dollarization on financial deepening by using different models and specifications while controlling for creditor rights and consumer credit information.

Using a sample of 44 developing countries with high dollar denominated deposits and different levels of inflation over the 1996–2002 period, the authors studied the effect of deposit dollarization (measured as the ratio dollar deposits to total bank deposits[2,3]) on the extent of financial deepening experienced by these countries (measured as the ratio of domestic credit extended by the banking system to the private sector to the GDP which is available from IMF's International Financial Statistics (IFS) database). The authors use a battery of models and estimation techniques in their analysis including Ordinary Least Squares (OLS) and Two-Stages-Least Squares to control for possible endogeneity issues as addressed by DeNicolo, Honohan and Ize (2005). The two equations estimated by the authors are:

$$\frac{CREDIT_{it}}{GDP_{it}} = \alpha + \beta_1 CRI_{it} + \beta_2 PB_{it} + \beta_3 INST_{it} + \beta_4 logCGDP_{it} + \beta_5 DDOLL_{it} + \beta_6 D_{it} * DDOLL_{it} + \beta_7 D_{it} + \varepsilon_{it} \quad (5.1)$$

$$\frac{CREDIT_{it}}{GDP_{it}} = \alpha + \beta_1 DDOLL_{it} + \beta_2 DDOLL_{it} * INF_{it} + \beta_3 INF_{it} + \beta_4 logCGDP_{it} + \varepsilon_{it} \quad (5.2)$$

Where $CREDIT_{it}$ is the domestic credit for country i in year t, GDP_{it} represents the nominal GDP in country i in year t and *CRI* is the creditor rights index which ranges from 0 (low protection) to 4 (high protection). This index shows the relative ease of seizing collateral by creditors if debt obligations are not fulfilled. The variable *PB* equals 1 if a private credit bureau operates in the country, 0 if otherwise. A private bureau is defined as a private commercial firm or non-profit organization that maintains a database on the standing of borrowers in the financial system, charged with

2 For robustness checks, the authors also used the ratio of foreign currency deposits in the banking system to the M2 money supply as their dollarization variable.

3 The amount of foreign exchange deposits in the banking system is obtained from Central Bank bulletins. For countries and years for which the data is not available from CB bulletins, the authors used the foreign currency deposit database compiled by Levy-Yeyati (2006).

the primary role of facilitating the exchange of information amongst banks and financial institutions. The variable *INST* is an equally-weighted average of the six institutional quality variables compiled by Kaufmann et al. (2009): Government Efficiency, Political Stability, Regulatory Quality, Rule of Law, Voice, and Corruption. The six governance indicators are measured in units ranging from –2.5 to 2.5, with higher values corresponding to better governance outcomes. Finally, $logCGDP_{it}$ is the logarithm of per capita income in country *i* in year *t*, and $DDOLL_{it}$ is the ratio of the dollar deposits in country *i* in year *t* to the overall deposits in the banking system. D_{it} is a dummy variable that takes the value of 1 if the inflation rate in country i in year t is over 20% and 0 if otherwise; $DDOLL_{it} * INF_{it}$ represents the interaction between dollarization and inflation; *INF* represents the natural logarithm of the inflation and ε is the error term.

The authors also use institutional quality variables as instruments in their estimations. The Creditor Rights Index (CRI) and Private Credit Bureau Availability Dummy (PB) are obtained from World Bank's *Doing Business* website.

Tables 5.1–5.3 show the authors' estimation results for the two models they used. Their results show that in countries with moderate inflationary processes, deposit dollarization consistently and significantly exerts a negative impact on financial deepening. This means that dollarization has a moderating effect on the adverse effects of inflation upon financial depth in high inflation economies.

In their paper, the authors also used the Minimum Variance Portfolio coefficient introduced by Ize and Levy-Yeyati (2003) and the Minimum Variance Portfolio coefficient calculated according to Neanidis and Savva (2009) (MVP2)[4] as analytical instruments. Tables 5.2 and 5.3 present these results.

From the Tables 5.2 and 5.3 the reader can extrapolate that, under different specifications, the authors verify that deposit dollarization does indeed have a negative impact on financial deepening in low inflation environments. This is consistent with the findings of De Nicolo, Honohan and Ize (2005), which show that dollarization moderates the negative effects of inflation on financial deepening under high inflation, but has pernicious effects on low-inflation economies. The coefficient of the dollarization variable ranges from −0.412 to −0.936 suggesting that a 10% increase in the deposit dollarization ratio can reduce the credit-to-GDP ratio by almost 4–9% in the countries studied. The value of the dollarization coefficient (DDOLL) is also much higher (in absolute value terms) in specifications where the Minimum Variance Portfolio variable defined according to Neanidis and Savva (2009) is used. (See Table 5.3).

In economies with controlled inflation, it appears that the dollarization of deposits in a banking system slows financial development by limiting domestic credit. These restrictions could be attributed to the currency mismatch and loan default risks

4 The authors define MVP in their analysis as $mvp = \sigma^2_{vt}/cov_{vut}$ where the numerator stands for the conditional variance of inflation and the denominator represents the conditional covariance between inflation and depreciation of the nominal exchange rate.

Table 5.1: Determinants of domestic private credit—all countries.

Dependent variable	**Domestic private credit to GDP**				
Method	OLS(1.1)	OLS(1.2)	OLS(1.3)	OLS(1.4)	OLS(1.5)
Time period	1990–2002	1990–2002	1990–2002	1990–2002	1996–2002
C	0.248***	0.190***	0.250***	0.259***	0.469***
	−0.024	−0.024	−0.033	−0.044	−0.066
CRI	0.102***	0.109***	0.093**	0.095***	0.106***
	−0.011	−0.011	−0.013	−0.014	−0.017
PB		0.255***	0.258***	0.258***	0.358***
		−0.033	−0.041	−0.041	−0.042
INST			0.140***	0.149***	0.136***
			−0.025	−0.038	−0.045
logCGDP				0.000	−0.000***
				0.000	0.000
DDOLL					−0.514***
					−0.067
D*DDOLL					0.487***
					−0.219
D					−0.294***
					−0.086
Adj. R square	0.105	0.178	0.274	0.273	0.397
Number of countries	56	56	54	54	44
Number of observations	637	637	377	377	274

Table 5.1 shows the estimation results of the first model (Eq. 5.1). CREDIT represents domestic credit, CGDP is the real per capita GDP in US Dollars, CRI is the creditor rights index which ranges from 0 (low protection) to 10 (high protection), INST stands for institutional quality and is an equally weighted average of the 6 institutional quality variables published by Kaufmann et al. (2009). It ranges from −2.5 to 2.5, with higher values corresponding to better governance outcomes. PB is a dummy variable that takes the value of 1 if there is a private credit bureau in the country, DDOLL is the ratio of the dollar deposits to the overall deposits in the banking system and D is the high-inflation dummy that takes the value of 1 if the inflation rate in country i in year t is over 20% and 0 otherwise. This table does not include the results for Africa and Middle East countries because the authors did not have a representative sample
*Significant at 10%; **significant at 5%; ***significant at 1%

that banking systems face in dollarized environments. Kutan, Ozsoz and Rengifo (2012) showed that dollarization exerts a negative impact on bank profitability and simultaneously contributes to the shallowness of the financial system.

The more foreign currency depositors want to keep in their bank accounts, the higher the risk banks face in terms of currency mismatches or loan defaults. In an effort to minimize their exposure to such risks, banks may find it in their best interests to be more careful in selecting their loan portfolios. As Court, Ozsoz and Rengifo (2012) put it, "Banks may scrutinize their credit applications more vigorously to make sure their borrowers have the ability to repay their loans independent of fluctuations in the value of the local currency and sometimes will not be willing to provide capital to good projects based on this exchange rate exposition" (p. 49).

However, when a country begins to experience the effects of high inflation,, dollarization plays a moderating effect on the adverse effects of inflation on financial

Table 5.2: Results of Model 2 using MVP.

Dependent variable:	**Domestic private credit to GDP**				
Method	OLS(2.1)	OLS(2.2)	TSLS(2.3)	TSLS(2.4)	TSLS(2.5)
Time period	1990–2004	1990–2004	1998–2004	1998–2004	1998–2004
C	0.732***	0.582***	0.708***	0.704***	0.067
	0.042	0.035	0.052	0.049	0.407
DDOLL	−0.412***				
	0.066				
DDOLL*INF		−0.098***	0.015	0.008	0.011
		0.04	0.014	0.014	0.014
INF	−0.059***	−0.022	−0.021***	−0.017***	−0.017***
	0.014	0.018	0.006	0.006	0.006
INST				0.155***	
				0.057	
logCGDP					0.088**
					0.004
INSTRUMENTS			A	A	B
Adj.R^2	0.099	0.043	0.123	0.196	0.169
Number of countries	47	47	23	23	23
Number of observations	461	461	107	107	107
SarganTest p value			0.822	0.023	0.015
Dependent variable:	**Domestic private credit to GDP**				
Method	TSLS(2.6)	OLS(2.7)	TSLS(2.8)	TSLS(2.9)	TSLS(2.10)
Time period	1998–2004	1990–2004	1998–2004	1998–2004	1998–2004
C	0.765***	0.919***	0.895***	0.866***	0.416
	0.065	0.057	0.076	0.075	0.432
DDOLL	−0.198	−0.936**	−0.604***	−0.522***	−0.542***
	0.138	0.13	0.188	0.189	0.196
DDOLL*INF		0.279***	0.060***	0.048***	0.053***
		0.06	0.199	0.02	0.02
INF	−0.16***	−0.157***	−0.035***	−0.030***	−0.032***
	0.004	0.025	0.007	0.057	0.008
INST				0.124***	
				0.057	
logCGDP					0.052
					0.046
INSTRUMENTS	**A**		**A**	**A**	**B**
Adj.R^2	0.147	0.137	0.217	0.252	0.227
Number of countries	23	47	23	23	23
Number of observations	107	461	107	107	107
SarganTest p value	0.03		0.05	0.06	0.09

Table 5.2 presents the results of the model developed by De Nicolo, Honohan and Ize (Eq. 5.2). DDOLL is the ratio of the dollar deposits to the overall deposits in the banking system, INF is the natural logarithm of the inflation, logCGDP is the logarithm of per capita GDP. Instrument list A: INST, MVP, RESTRIC Instrument List B: A + logCGDP. Where INST stands for institutional quality, MVP the Minimum Variance Portfolio coefficient, RESTRIC the index of restrictions on the holdings of foreign currency deposits. The null for the Sargan test: The error term is uncorrelated with the instruments. The critical values for chi2(2) and chi2(3) are 5.991 and 7.815 at 5% critical value.
*Significant at 10%; **significant at 5%; ***significant at 1%

Table 5.3: Results of Model 2 using MVP2.

Dependent variable:	**Domestic private credit to GDP**				
Method	OLS(2.1)	OLS(2.2)	TSLS(2.3)	TSLS(2.4)	TSLS(2.5)
Time period	1990–2004	1990–2004	1998–2004	1998–2004	1998–2004
C	0.732***	0.582***	0.588***	0.601***	0.36
	0.042	0.035	0.035	0.034	0.327
DDOLL	−0.412***				
	0.066				
DDOLL*INF		−0.098***	−0.002	−0.083	−0.003
		0.009	0.058	0.009	0.056
INF	−0.059***	−0.022	−0.009*	−0.036	−0.006
	0.014	0.018	0.004	0.004	0.032
INST				0.176***	
				0.044	
logCGDP					0.118***
					0.037
INSTRUMENTS			A	A	B
Adj.R2	0.099	0.043	0.069	0.146	0.125
Number of countries	47	47	40	40	40
Number of observations	461	461	180	180	170
SarganTest p value			0.07	0.07	0.216
Dependent variable:	**Domestic private credit to GDP**				
Method	TSLS(2.6)	OLS(2.7)	TSLS(2.8)	TSLS(2.9)	TSLS(2.10)
Time period	1998–2004	1990–2004	1998–2004	1998–2004	1998–2004
C	0.756***	0.919***	0.880***	0.863***	0.193
	0.049	0.057	0.057	0.056	0.301
DDOLL	−0.456***	−0.936**	−0.746***	−0.674***	−0.673***
	0.096	0.13	0.121	0.12	0.124
DDOLL*INF		0.279***	0.042***	0.042***	0.035***
		0.06	0.011	0.011	0.011
INF	−0.101***	−0.157***	−0.028***	−0.024***	−0.024***
	0.002	0.025	0.04	0.005	0.005
INST				0.132***	
				0.041	
logCGDP					0.077**
					0.033
INSTRUMENTS	A		A	A	B
Adj.R^2	0.165	0.137	0.234	0.259	0.257
Number of countries	40	47	40	40	40
Number of observations	180	461	180	180	180
SarganTest p value	0.02		0.36	0.66	0.822

Table 5.3 presents the results of the model developed by De Nicolo, Honohan and Ize (2005) according to their Equation (5.2). DDOLL is the ratio of the dollar deposits to the overall deposits in the banking system, INF is the natural logarithm of the inflation, logCGDP is the logarithm of per capita GDP. Instrument list A: INST, MVP, RESTRIC Instrument List B: A + logCGDP. Where INST stands for institutional quality, MVP2 the Minimum Variance Portfolio coefficient calculated according to Neanidis and Savva (2009), RESTRIC the index of restrictions on the holdings of foreign currency deposits. The null for the Sargan test: Over identification restrictions are not valid. The critical values for chi^2 (2) and chi^2 (3) are 5.991 and 7.815 at 5% critical value.
*Significant at 10%; **significant at 5%; ***significant at 1%.

depth of an economy, as indicated by the sign of the interaction term (DDOLL * INF) in Tables 5.1 through 5.3. This finding is also consistent with the findings of De Nicolo, Honohan and Ize (2005). This result could be linked to previously discussed role of dollarization as an alternative hedging mechanism for savings.

Court, Ozsoz and Rengifo (2012) found that inflation (INF) by itself has a negative and significant coefficient on financial deepening. This is an expected result. High inflation restricts the availability of credit in an economy. The coefficient of the inflation variable (INF) varies between −0.03 and −0.16, meaning that a 1% increase in the inflation rate lowers the credit-to-GDP ratio in the countries studied between 0.03 and 0.16%. Additionally, the variable that accounts for institutional quality (INST) has a positive and significant coefficient around 0.15, suggesting that a one-step increase in the value of this variable increases credit-to-GDP ratio by 15%. The results gathered at the regional level also support this view; the authors explain that "this result is not surprising given that previous literature (such as Graff (2003) among others) has demonstrated that institutional quality and culture are important in the financial development of transition and emerging market economies" (p. 50). A graphical illustration of these findings can be found in Figures 5.5 and 5.6.

Figure 5.7 shows dollarization (measured as the ratio of dollar deposits to M2 money supply) and financial depth ratios (measured as the ratio of domestic credit to GDP) for selected dollarized economies.

For highly dollarized economies, the trend line that shows the relationship between dollarization and financial deepening is steeper as opposed to the overall sample. The slope coefficient equals 0.426 and is statistically significant at the 5% level.

Figure 5.8 presents a scatter diagram charting the relationship between financial depth and deposit dollarization rates for 9 heavily dollarized economies in this sample. We define a heavy dollarized economy as an economy where the ratio of foreign currency deposits to M2 is more than 30%.

5.3 Financial Inclusion

The topic of financial inclusion studies the relationship between the financial deepening of an economy and growth rates, and refers to the availability of financial products (deposits, savings, loans, etc.) and the ease of access to these products by most economic agents in an economy. Dollarization and financial inclusion bear some relation; in economies where foreign currency accounts are available, more individuals can enjoy access to credit lines in foreign currencies in addition to the local currency. As a corollary, dollarization may have a positive impact on financial inclusion,[5] and one would expect financial markets that exhibit some of the characteristics of dollarization to be more inclusive.

5 More research is need and the authors are working on related questions.

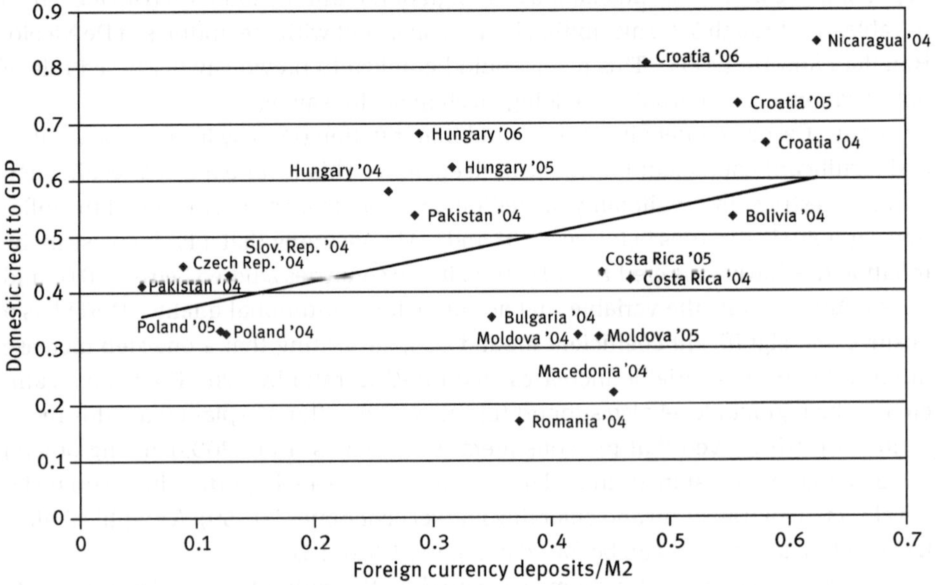

Figure 5.7: Financial depth vs dollarization in selected dollarized economies.
The figure shows financial depth (measured as the ratio of domestic credit to GDP) of several economies versus its deposit dollarization (measured as the ratio dollar deposits to M2). The equation for the fitted line is Credit-to-GDP=0.426*Dollarization+0.33.
Source: IMF-IFS, Court, Ozsoz and Rengifo (2012).

In this section we highlight the possible relationships that one can deduce from examining common economic-financial data. Table 5.4 shows the dollarization and bank account ownership ratios for the ten countries that have the highest bank account ownership percentages among low, middle and upper middle income countries, as ranked by the World Bank. According to the table, except for Thailand, Mauritius and Sri Lanka all of the countries in the list can be considered heavily dollarized, since their respective dollarization ratio is above 20%.

The financial instruments that we refer to in this section are the possibility of opening banking accounts (savings) and the availability of access to different loan or credit products (investment loans, consumption credit, mortgages, among others) in both local and foreign denominated currencies.

Economic agents in several developing economies (especially agents in frontier markets[6]) do not have access to the full array of financial instruments available

6 "Frontier market economies are more developed than the least developed economies, but are still too small to be considered emerging markets. Many of them lack proper financial development and institutional strength, making them vulnerable to factors that can deteriorate economic stability or exacerbate fluctuations" (Glebocki-Keefe, Rengifo and Trendafilov 2015).

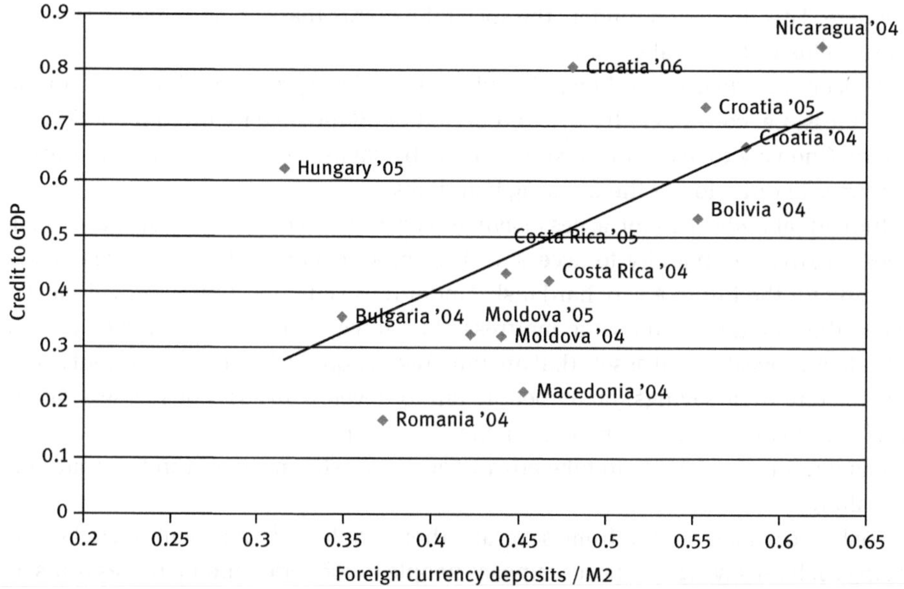

Figure 5.8: Financial depth vs dollarization in selected dollarized economies (heavily dollarized economies).
The figure shows the financial depth of an economy (measured as the ratio of domestic credit to GDP) versus its deposit dollarization (measured as the ratio dollar deposits to total bank deposits) in heavily dollarized economies (where the ratio of foreign currency deposits to the M2 is more than 30%). The equation for the fitted line is Credit-to-GDP=1.45*Dollarization+0.18.
Source: IMF-IFS, Court, Ozsoz and Rengifo (2012).

Table 5.4: Financial inclusion and dollarization.

Country name	Account at a financial institution, older adults (% ages 25+, as of 2014)	Dollarization ratio (%)	Dollarization metric used	Inflation rate (as of 2014, annual) (%)
Iran, Islamic Rep.	93.5	NA		17.2
Latvia	91.6	92.7	±	0.6
Mongolia	91.4	24.7	**	13.0
Lithuania	86.9	34.0	**	0.1
Mauritius	85.4	13.5	***	3.8
Serbia	83.8	NA		2.1
Sri Lanka	82.0	11.3	*	3.3
Malaysia	82.0	25.1	**	3.1
Jamaica	79.9	37.5	***	8.3
Thailand	79.8	1.3	***	1.9

Table 5.4 shows the dollarization ratios and bank account ownership for the countries that rank within the top ten among World Bank's list of low, middle and upper middle income countries in terms of financial inclusion. The dollarization metrics used are: *Liability Dollarization, **Foreign Currency Deposit to M2, ***Foreign Currency deposits to Total Deposits, ± Loan Dollarization (Ratio of Foreign Currency Loans to total Loans.
Source: World Bank Financial Inclusion Database (Findex), IMF—Financial Soundness Indicators (FSI), IMF—International Financial Statistics, Yeyati (2006) and Kutan, Ozsoz and Rengifo (2012).

elsewhere. This limitation hinders the societal benefits that can be achieved through a more inclusive financial sector.

As economic theory has shown, individuals display a preference for consumption smoothness, i.e. consumers try to avoid period of abundance followed by periods of scarcity. One way to avoid those situations is by saving economic resources during good times in order to use them during bad times.

Individuals who cannot access savings accounts face many problematic challenges. Firstly, the inability to access savings products and related services makes preparing for the future a very hard task. Under these circumstances, individuals try to keep their moneys "under the mattress" (a strategy with obvious drawbacks) or alternatively invest in real assets that are not always liquid.[7,8] Secondly, without a safe place to store their savings, many people fail to develop any sort of saving strategy at all.[9] Thirdly, individuals who are unable to save or access other financial services such as lending are unable to take advantage of investment opportunities that may come along.

Cash economies suffer from several other problems.[10] As mentioned before, keeping cash for savings purposes exposes people to robberies and increases transactional costs. For example, performing cash transactions that involve large amounts or are executed between parties located far away from one another presents additional security risks and coordination problems. Overall, it is clear that economic agents in developing countries could benefit greatly from broad, low-cost access to financial services provided by the banking systems.

As a way to show access to the financial services commonly available in developed economies, Figure 5.9 shows ten countries within World Bank's low, middle and upper middle income group (a total of 112 countries) that have the highest credit card ownership ratios for individuals above the age of 15 years old.

As can be seen even in the countries with the highest penetration ratios (Uruguay and Turkey) this number does not go above 40%. In the meantime, in the US this ratio

---

7 Liquidity is defined as how easily an asset can be converted to cash with the lowest price impact for the seller. In the case of real assets acquired as an alternative to saving (mostly in emerging markets poor and rural populations), these assets are usually difficult to liquidate) without a significant discount. This implies that in many cases, this saving substitute is far from being a perfect, at least in liquidity terms.

8 Some individuals in developing countries (mostly poor and rural citizens) may have significant wealth in certain physical assets like livestock or jewelry. Although these tangible assets can be useful for preserving net worth over time, they have significant disadvantages in terms of liquidity and security when compared with banking accounts. For example, livestock are vulnerable to disease, jewelry is vulnerable to theft, and neither enjoys the divisibility effects of currency.

9 This can potentially affect not only long-term but short-term planning. Limited access to financial instruments can extend to being unable to obtain medical insurance or pensions, for example.

10 The World Bank shows that 420 million unbanked adults receive government wages or transfer payments in cash. 440 million unbanked farmers receive cash payments for the sale of agricultural products.

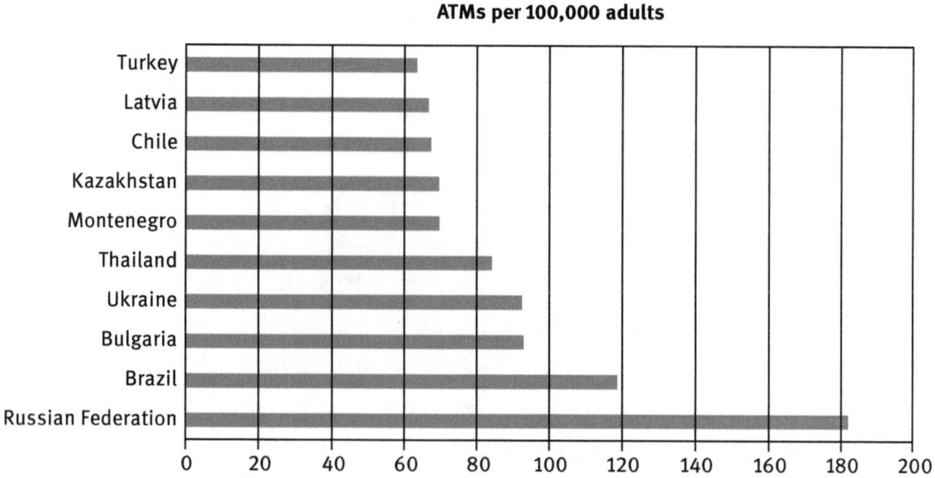

Figure 5.9: Top ten low, middle and upper middle income countries in terms of ATMs per 100,000 (2014). Source: World Bank, Findex Database.

is over 60% and in Canada (which has the highest number of ATMs per capita as of 2014), this ratio reaches 77%. (Source: Findex Database, World Bank).

Other metrics used to examine financial inclusion are presented in Figures 5.10 (top ten developing countries with the highest percentage of adults that have borrowed from a financial institution in 2014) and 5.11 (Bottom ten developing countries

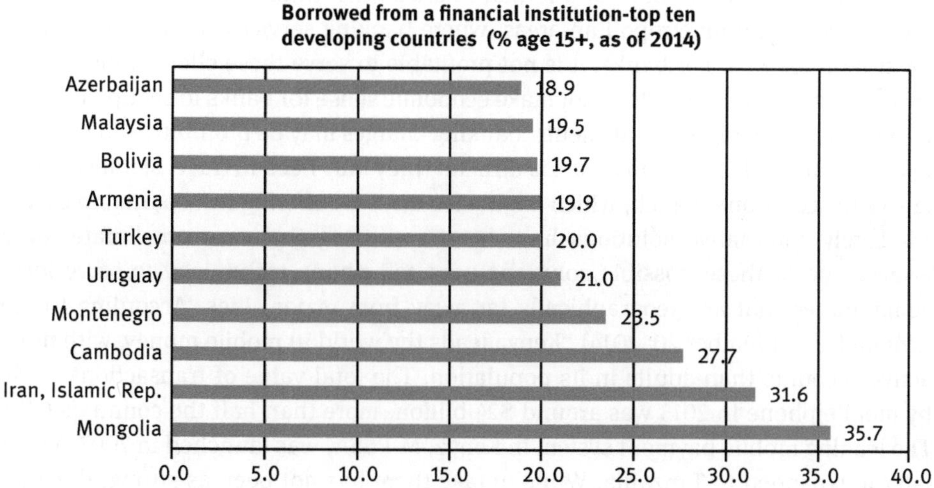

Figure 5.10: Top ten low, middle and upper-middle income countries in terms of the percentage of adults that have borrowed from a financial institution in 2014.
Source: World Bank, Findex Database.

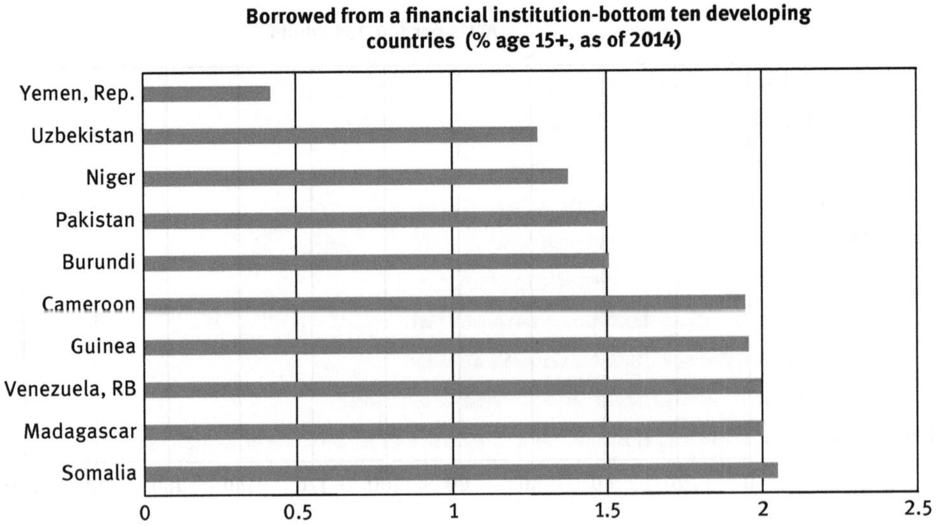

Figure 5.11: Bottom ten low, middle and upper middle income countries in terms of percentage of adults that have borrowed from a financial institution in 2014.
Source: World Bank, Findex Database.

with the lowest percentage of adults that have borrowed from a financial institution) as well as in Table 5.5 (credit depth index). These two metrics are used to show often economic agents access lines of credit (Figure 5.12).

According to the World Bank financial inclusion data,[11] there are two billion people who do not have an account at a formal financial institution. This problem is more pronounced in non-metropolitan areas, where banking services cannot be provided for several reasons. For banks, it is not profitable to serve these clients (due to high monitoring costs), thus it does not make economic sense for banks to set up branches in such places. For individual clients, banking charges may be prohibitive, and access to their local bank branch may be too difficult (they may need to travel significant distances to access one branch, which might also involve suffering transportation costs).

Lately, alternative solutions have been appearing that may ameliorate these issues. One of these possible solutions uses cell phone technology to serve local communities that are geographically far away from major cities. According to the Economist (September 20, 2014) "Kenya leads the world in mobile money, with more active accounts than adults in its population. The total value of transactions made by mobile phone in 2013 was around $24 billion, more than half the country's GDP. The leading mobile payment system in Kenya, M-PESA, was launched in 2007. A year later it expanded to Tanzania. While uptake there has not been as strong, the total

11 http://datatopics.worldbank.org/financialinclusion/

Table 5.5: Low, middle and upper-middle income countries with the highest ranking of credit depth information index (as of 2014).

Country name	Depth of credit information index (0=low to 8=high)
Benchmarks	
USA	8
Germany	8
China	6
Euro Area	5.68
Developing countries with highest scores	
Argentina	8
Armenia	8
Dominican Republic	8
Ecuador	8
Egypt, Arab Rep.	8
Georgia	8
Honduras	8
Lithuania	8
Mexico	8
Nicaragua	8
Panama	8
Paraguay	8
Peru	8
Uruguay	8
Middle-ranking countries	
Bulgaria	5
Cambodia	5
Kyrgyz Republic	5
Latvia	5
Lebanon	5
Philippines	5
Tunisia	5
Countries with the lowest scores	
Afghanistan	0
Algeria	0
Angola	0
Bangladesh	0
Belize	0
Burkina Faso	0
Burundi	0
Central African Republic	0
Chad	0
Comoros	0
Congo, Dem. Rep.	0
Cote d'Ivoire	0
Djibouti	0
Ethiopia	0
Guinea	0

Table 5.5: (continued)

Country name	Depth of credit information index (0=low to 8=high)
Haiti	0
Iraq	0
Jordan	0
Kenya	0
Lao PDR	0
Lesotho	0
Liberia	0
Madagascar	0
Malawi	0
Mali	0
Mauritania	0
Myanmar	0
Nepal	0
Niger	0
Senegal	0
Sierra Leone	0
Sudan	0
Tanzania	0
Togo	0
Uganda	0
Yemen, Rep.	0

Source: World Bank Findex Database.

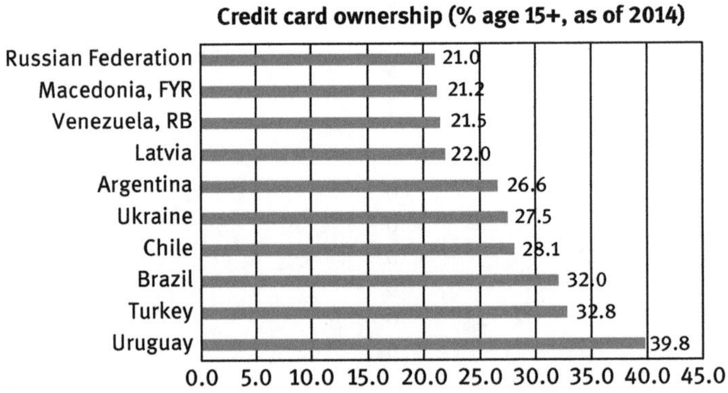

Figure 5.12: Credit card ownership: top ten countries among low, middle and upper-middle income group.
Figure 5.12 shows the ten countries within World Bank's low, middle and upper middle income group (a total of 112 countries) that have the highest credit card ownership ratios for individuals above 15 years of age.
Source: Findex Database, World Bank.

transaction value is close to that of Kenya. As mobile phones have become more widely available, mobile payment transfers have helped reach the 'unbanked'. In at least eight countries, including Congo and Zimbabwe, more people have registered mobile-money accounts than traditional bank accounts" (Figure 5.13).

A pioneer service called M-Pesa (Kenya) allows customers to use simple cell phone technology (SMS messaging) to make payments through mobile phones. M-Pesa has also become a popular method of sending remittances from urban to rural areas.

Similarly to M-Pesa, there are several companies in different countries that have been experimenting with these technologies to make banking services available to many people in different geographic regions. Amongst these we have bKash in Bangladesh, GCash and SMART Money in the Philippines.

Recently, cell phones have been exploiting internet-technologies (smart phones); thanks to economies of scale, falling commodity prices and burgeoning expertise, the costs to manufacture smart phones are falling, and supporting these technological advances, internet service payments are also being reduced significantly. This is allowing more and more people access to smart phones, enabling service providers to extend their reach and further invest in infrastructure to service this growing demand.

The increasing availability of smart phones at lower prices and with cheaper connectivity fees can greatly facilitate financial transactions and improve the ease of access to financial products in developing countries.[12]

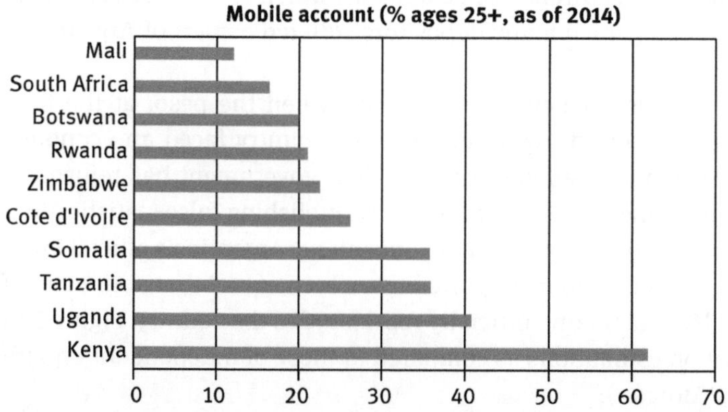

Figure 5.13: Mobile money in developing countries (top ten in terms of account ownership, 2014). Figure 5.13 shows the ten countries with the highest mobile account holder ratios as a percentage of adult population (aged 25 and older) among the low, middle and upper middle income group countries.
Source: Findex Database, World Bank.

12 A topic that is out the reach of the book that however is important to mention is the more frequent use of digital currencies like bitcoins and bit shares. These digital currencies are now being used to increase banking services and to facilitate international trade.

5.4 Bitcoin: The New Future Form of Dollarization?

First appearing in 2008, Bitcoin is one of the first digital or crypto-currencies. Bitcoin is the world's first fully decentralized, peer-to-peer system for electronic transactions.

Bitcoin facilitates the transfer of value between two unknown parties without relying on a third party to validate the transaction. Bitcoin has eliminated the need for a centralized clearing house (i.e. credit card company, bank, government, or escrow agent) allowing monetary transfers that are approved through a mechanism that involves the entire network but does not rely on any single individual or institution. In this environment, banks and governments have no power to create bitcoins, and nobody can freeze or seize funds that do not belong to them.

Paying for a good or service can be done almost instantly, anywhere in the world via an internet connection. Bitcoin has the potential to alter the world's economic landscape, and its related technologies could potentially offer solutions to unbanked and under-banked individuals and improve the stuttering economies in which they live. Argentina is a clear example of a country where Bitcoin has become increasingly popular due to structural economic problems and capital controls.

Argentina was rated by Bloomberg as one of the worst economies in the world in 2015 (Bloomberg News); the government's strategies to solve the country's economic problems have proved extremely inefficient in reducing unemployment and controlling inflation. In this environment, out-of-the-box solutions are appearing, and among them we can find digital currencies like bitcoins, which are out of the reach of forced currency conversions (which many depositors suffered as part of Argentina's slew of capital controls).

Argentina faced a serious financial crisis in 2001 when the peso, at the time pegged to the US dollar, collapsed. Again in 2014, the country faced an economic crisis and government responses failed once more. The government has refused to acknowledge the extremely high levels of inflation by publishing false statistics that contradict studies conducted by independent organizations. Argentina's official inflation figures had been massaged and misreported to such an extent that at the end of 2013, the International Monetary Fund officially reprimanded the country. Figure 5.14 shows the official inflation estimations as compared to those of independent organizations estimated by JP Morgan):

Facing this crisis, Argentinian confidence in the peso is very low. Most of Argentina's citizens prefer US dollars to protect their purchasing power. However, citizens can only convert portion of their income to USD due to government regulations. Also, as mentioned previously, dollar purchases are taxed up to 20%.

The Argentinian government has also imposed capital controls in an attempt to reduce the capital outflows from the country. This, together with citizens' restrictions to buy dollars, has created a growing black market for foreign currencies, especially US dollars. As shown in Chapter 1, the spread between the unofficial (black market)

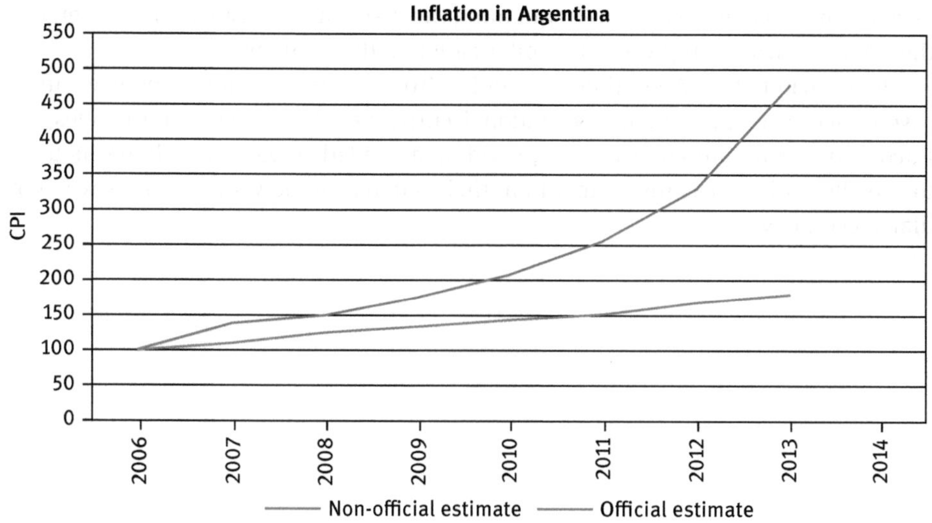

Figure 5.14: Inflation in Argentina official vs unofficial figures.
Source: JP Morgan/FT.

and official rates is large. Furthermore, all black market transactions are done in cash, which leaves Argentinians vulnerable to theft or fraud.

When citizens no longer believe in the credibility of the government and financial institutions, individuals desire a method to circumvent traditionally sanctioned institutions and avoid government interference. Consequently, many people in Argentina are currently using Bitcoin as a way to circumvent the traditional financial system.

Online retailer "Avalancha" introduced the option to pay with Bitcoin. The company is able to offer a 10% discount to customers who pay with Bitcoin, as the cost efficiency of Bitcoin allows them to earn more on these transactions than they would on credit card transactions processed through the banking system.

Moreover, during the summer of 2014, Argentina-based Bitcoin company Bit-Pagos launched its "Ripio" service that enables users to buy bitcoins at more than 8,000 mobile phone kiosks and allowing customers to buy small amounts of bitcoin at convenience stores within the kiosks. This makes it much easier for Argentinians to purchase Bitcoins, as the country's regulations prohibit individuals from purchasing bitcoins through online exchanges.

More importantly, customers can use this service without having a bank account. If a customer has access to a kiosk, the transaction can be executed using just a mobile phone. This allows potential customers to utilize digital currencies while circumventing existing financial institutions entirely. Moreover, as accessing bitcoins becomes more convenient than frequenting the black market, Bitcoin will emerge as the primary currency representing dollarization in the economy.

It is obvious that Argentina is suffering from failed government policies and a severe lack of confidence in the national currencies. Here, digital currencies like Bitcoin infrastructure appear to be providing a needed service that allows its users to use alternative measures to maintain their purchasing power under a heavily regulated economy.

6 Policy Interventions in Dollarized Economies

6.1 Introduction

Formulating and executing monetary policy in a partially dollarized economy is a demanding process for central bankers.

Up to this point, the reader should understand the following. First, movements in exchange rates and inflation rates are closely related, more so in highly dollarized economies. Furthermore, as explained by Alvarez-Plata and Garca-Herrero (2008), in highly dollarized economies there is stronger exchange rate pass-through, since many non-traded goods are priced in foreign currency, making their prices highly sensitive to exchange rate fluctuations.

Second, dollarization occurs not only in periods of high inflation, but also when economic agents lose trust in their policymakers and institutions. Strong institutional quality is critical in explaining why some countries have been able to decrease their dollarization numbers faster than those with weak institutions, even though both countries have been able to significantly reduce and manage inflation.

Third, currency mismatch risks on banks' balance sheets increases the sensitivity of the small open and partially dollarized economy to changes in exchange rates. Volatile flows can lead to balance sheet risks and bank failures, increasing hedging costs and the possibility of default risks.

Thus, under dollarization, the banking system faces risks that do not materialize in non-dollarized economies, as was discussed in detail in Chapter 4. Intriguingly, even though dollarization appears as a rational response to instabilities of local currencies (inflationary and hyper inflationary processes), it is not yet clear why dollarization levels do not decrease (or at least do not decrease at a faster rate) when the local currency achieves stability and economic growth is apparent (see possible explanations in Chapter 3).

It is also widely recognized that although dollarization can create some macroeconomic stability in periods of high inflation, it is also a main source of potential liquidity and solvency crises. It is for this reason that current research is increasingly focused on the risks associated with partial dollarization, as a way to understand its impact on monetary policy conducted by many central banks and monetary authorities.

In this chapter, we start by presenting the ways in which monetary authorities intervene in foreign exchange markets in order to decrease exchange rate volatility. We start by recognizing several of the risks faced by the banks; these were fully described in Chapter 4. Recall that one of the main risks faced by banks and society in general arises from the efforts of the banking industry to decrease foreign currency risks originating from their asset and liability imbalances.

As we have discussed, a natural hedge against this type of asset risk is to create liabilities denominated in the same foreign currency. However, by doing this, banks increase their default risks. This action also contributes to the instability that economic systems face in distressed periods. Sudden depreciations or appreciations of the local currency can change the value of a bank's liabilities or assets, can increase the real value of borrowers' (households, corporations and government) debt, and can pose systemic risks that must be addressed.

In this chapter, we discuss how monetary authorities in partially dollarized economies steer their monetary policies in such troublesome environments. We look at some case studies where central bank policies are designed to account for volatile foreign currency fluctuations. We also look at some of the regulatory changes in dollarized economies as a result of the 2008–2009 Global Financial Crisis and discuss the reasons why these countries have taken such measures.

The chapter is organized as follows. Section 6.2 discusses the challenges of conducting monetary policy in partially dollarized economies. Section 6.3 analyzes the changes in regulatory attitudes after the financial crisis by providing theoretical frameworks and research findings exploring the case of Turkey, a heavily dollarized economy which changed its regulatory approach to dollarization in the aftermath of the Global Financial Crisis.

6.2 Monetary Policy in Partially Dollarized Economies

The inclusion of foreign currency into a country's money supply complicates or reduces the monetary policy options available to central bankers and policy makers. This happens partly as a result of policy makers' (in dollarized economies) utilization of other forms of economic and financial tools in formulating and setting their monetary policies. For instance, in determining the changes in reserves required from depository institutions, policy makers consider not only the local currency but also foreign currency deposits and reach a decision accordingly.

It is important to note that a central focus of monetary policy is to ensure price stability,[1] is one of the main conditions for encouraging sustainable and inclusive growth and for creating employment. However, and as was mentioned in Chapter 3, there is a clear relationship between exchange rates and inflation. It is due to this connection that almost 65% of the IMF's members publish data on foreign exchange interventions (IMF, 2010). Thus, besides considering traditional monetary policies, it is important for policymakers in partially dollarized economies also to consider exchange rate policies.

As shown by Acosta-Ormaechea and Coble (2011), the exchange rate channel is a more relevant consideration than the traditional interest rate channel when targeting inflation in highly dollarized economies. Again, the transmission mechanism from the exchange rate channel to inflation targeting policies may be due to the stronger exchange rate pass-through in dollarized economies.

1 In general, another goal is output growth (see for example the well-known Taylor rule).

The same results are obtained by Carranza, Galdon-Sanchez and Gomez-Biscarri (2009), who find that the negative balance sheet effects resulting from the depreciation of a currency are stronger in highly dollarized economies. They explain this significantly stronger transmission mechanism by arguing that the degree of dollarization has a high impact on the pass-through between inflation and exchange rates. They argue that a real depreciation event increases the relative prices of imported goods, exerting an upward influence in the inflation contingent on the share of imports in consumption spending.

In their paper, the authors also mention that in highly dollarized economies, corporations as well as banks experience weakening of their balance sheets due to the currency mismatches. These currency mismatches may not only affect the investment decisions taken by firms, but also may negatively impact aggregate demand, leading to a contraction in output. Thus, the transfer of exchange rate movements to fluctuations in inflation rates is more profound in highly dollarized economies.

In an economy where a good portion of savings and loans are held in foreign currency, sudden changes in the exchange rate cause pockets of instability in the financial system that can spread to affect the whole economy. As a result, monetary authorities monitor exchange rates more closely, and might have to intervene in times of turbulence to provide stability to the system (through reducing exchange rate volatility and exerting countercyclical policies to reverse exchange rate trends not based on fundamentals).

Therefore, it has been argued that central bank policies differ according to the degree and type of dollarization they face. For example, central banks in highly dollarized economies might try to protect the banking system from sudden exchange rate changes by actively participating in the currency markets. By doing so, monetary authorities expect to avoid a potential crisis that could occur due to a lack of liquidity in the banking sector, which could lead to bank runs. To this end, Ozsoz, Rengifo and Salvatore (2010) studied central bank behavior in three transition economies (Czech Republic, Croatia and Slovakia) with varying degrees of dollarization to see if central bank interventions in the currency markets can be predicted as an outcome of exchange rate fluctuations. They hypothesized that "central banks in highly dollarized economies would try to protect the banking system from sudden exchange rate changes by actively participating in the currency markets in order to avoid a potential crisis that could occur due to banks' lack of liquidity." (p. 6). For this purpose, the following framework was created:

$$inter_{it} = \alpha_i + \rho_i erv_{it} + \beta_i movav_{it} + \varepsilon_{it} \tag{6.1}$$

where $inter_{it}$ is a dummy variable that represents central bank intervention in country i at time t, erv_{it} represents the volatility of the real effective exchange rate (REER), movavit is the moving average of the REER for the past 12 month period and ε_{it} is a mean zero, constant variance disturbance term, assumed to be normally distributed.

The authors estimate Eq. (6.1) by using a probit model where $inter_{it}$ takes the value "0" if there is no central bank intervention in the forex market and "1" if there is an intervention. They also use this model to study whether there are asymmetries in central bank interventions when purchases and sales of foreign currency by the central bank are considered separately. In this case, the endogenous variable takes on the value of 1 when the central bank intervention involved buying or selling foreign currency, and 0 if there was no intervention at all.

To test their hypothesis, the authors used data on the amount of foreign exchange deposits in the banking systems obtained by examining the Central Bank Bulletins of each of the three countries. The dollarization measure they use is the average ratio of the foreign exchange deposits in the country's banking institutions to the country's M2 money supply for the period. They construct a monthly index for central bank's announced dates of intervention in the foreign exchange market by reading each central bank's annual reports.

The most comprehensive datasets for central bank interventions in their sample were for the Slovak and Czech Republics for the 1998–2006 period. For Croatia, their sample is much shorter, covering the period 2005–2006. Among the three economies studied, Croatia is the most dollarized economy (with an average dollarization of 51.9% for the 2005–2006 period for which the authors conducted their estimations). The other two countries, the Czech Republic, and the Slovak Republic, had average dollar-denominated deposits of 10.5% and 14.3% to their M2 respectively for the 1998–2004 period. Furthermore, all three economies have low and controlled inflation rates.[2]

During the authors' observation period of 24 months (2005–2006), the Croatian Central Bank intervened in the foreign exchange markets 13 times, averaging one intervention less than every two months, while for the Slovak Republic the central bank intervened on average once per 13 months (from 1998 to 2006). In the case of the Czech Republic, the Czech National Bank intervened in the country's foreign currency markets in 16 months of the 60-month period between 1998 and 2006, with most of these interventions taking place between 1998 and 2002. Table 6.1 presents the results of the authors' probit estimations.

As can be seen in Table 6.1, the only variable that has an explanatory power in all cases is the volatility of the REER (ERV). The strength of the coefficient is stronger for Croatia, the most heavily dollarized economy in the author's sample. In all of the cases, the sign of the exchange rate volatility is the expected one, meaning that a higher volatility implies a higher probability of a central bank intervention. For both the Czech Republic and the Slovak Republic, the moving average of the REER of the last 12 months (a proxy for the long term REER) is statistically significant.

2 The average inflation rates between 1998 and 2006 are 3.55%, 3.38%, and 7.02% for Croatia, the Czech Republic and Slovak Republic, respectively

Table 6.1: Probability of Central Bank Intervention—Croatia, Czech Republic, and Slovak Republic.

Dependent variable:	**Central Bank Intervention (*inter*)**		
Country	Croatia	Czech Rep.	Slovak Rep.
Period	2005–2006	1998–2006	1998–2006
ERV	6.34***	0.48***	0.10*
	(2.10)	(0.26)	(0.03)
REER Moving Av	−0.13	−0.13**	−0.13**
	(0.33)	(0.05)	(0.06)
McFadden R^2	0.22	0.27	0.14
No of observations	24	97	97
LR Stat	7.40(0.06) *	9.56(0.0002) ***	13.39(0.003) ***

Table 6.1 presents the results of probit estimations of the probability of direct central banks' intervention in the foreign currency markets. The table comes from Ozsoz, Rengifo and Salvatore (2010). The dependent variable is the dummy for central bank intervention observed at monthly intervals; takes on the value of 1 if there is a central bank intervention during the period and 0 otherwise. ERV is volatility of the local currency exchange rate. REER Moving Av is the 12 month moving average of the REER. For Croatia we use the 6-month ERV instead of the 12-month one due to statistical significance of the first. Standard errors are presented in parenthesis except for the LR Stat that corresponds to its corresponding p-value.
*means significant at 10%, **significant at 5% and, ***significant at 1%.

The authors also find that central banks are more likely to intervene in currency markets when there are higher risks of currency mismatches in partially dollarized economies.

Using probit and ordered-choice models, the authors establish that for the three economies examined, real exchange rate volatility and the moving average of the real effective exchange rate (REER) significantly explain direct central bank interventions into foreign currency markets.

As illustrated in Figure 6.1, the authors show that almost 70% of the foreign exchange interventions by the Croatian National Bank were correctly accounted for. For the Czech Republic case, 16.67% of interventions and 98.8% of non-interventions were adequately forecasted and, for Slovakia 17.5% of interventions and 98.75% of non-interventions were correctly predicted. The findings of this paper suggest that foreign exchange rate volatility and trends are important benchmarks for regulators in dollarized economies, and therefore have an important informational role that helps regulators to formulate their monetary and exchange rate policies.

6.3 Regulatory Attitudes Toward Dollarization in the Aftermath of the Financial Crisis

The Global Financial Crisis of 2008–2009 was a good opportunity for academics and policy makers to see whether the threats posed by the dollarization of bank deposits and loans hold in practice.

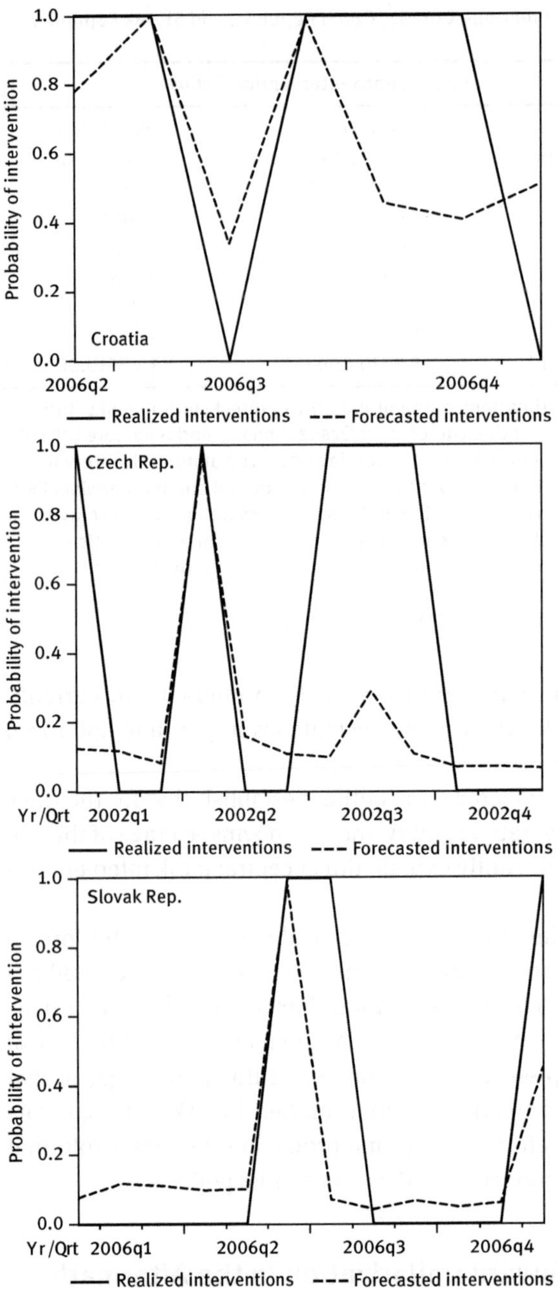

Figure 6.1: Probabilities of real versus forecasted central bank intervention in Croatia, Czech Republic, and Slovak Republic.

Figure 6.1 shows the forecasted probability of a direct central bank intervention and compares it with actual interventions. The dependent variable is the dummy for central banks' intervention observed at monthly intervals; it takes the value 1 if there is a central bank intervention during the period and 0 otherwise.

Since then, a number of studies have evaluated the economic consequences of partial dollarization in the countries' banking sectors. Among this body of research, one of the noteworthy studies was performed by Chithu (2012), who finds that for 60 emerging economies, unofficial dollarization/euroization was an important contributor to the severity of the financial crisis. His research showed that real GDP contracted by around 0.84 more percentage points in economies where loan dollarization was 10 percentage points or higher. Additionally, the author finds that "the adverse impact of dollarization/euroization has been transmitted through all the main channels traditionally highlighted in the literature, i.e. currency mismatches, reduced monetary policy autonomy and limited lender of last resort ability, all of which became more binding constraints in the midst of the crisis."

The restrictive impact of dollarization on monetary policy was also mentioned in other studies. For instance, Velickovski and Pugh (2011), who investigated the pass-through effects of exchange rate to domestic prices in a study of 23 developed and 12 transition economies, found that euroization (or dollarization) restricts monetary policy in transition economies with high levels of euroization (or dollarization) through its effect on exchange rate policy.[3] The authors mention that there is a higher exchange-rate pass through to consumer prices in transition economies than in developed economies and attribute this finding to high levels of euroization, which provide "more direct channels between exchange rate changes and price changes" (p. 4123).

The regulatory actions taken by the governments and central banks of some of the most highly dollarized economies also confirm these findings. Following the Global Financial Crisis, regulators in Hungary, Latvia and Poland have tightened eligibility requirements for borrowing in foreign currency and have encouraged banks to use moral suasion to deter retail level foreign currency borrowing. The authorities in these countries require banks to clearly disclose the exchange rate risks of foreign currency loans to their clients.

In countries like Croatia, Kazakhstan and Romania, stronger provisioning requirements were also imposed on foreign currency lending (Brown and Haas, 2012). Ukraine completely banned foreign currency lending to households in late 2008.

In June 2010, the European Central Bank (ECB) stated that national efforts to rein in FX lending in eastern European economies have had little impact, and therefore called for coordinated efforts to be taken by EU member states. Among these efforts, they requested that regulators from banks' home countries which own subsidiaries in Eastern Europe restrict their foreign currency lending (Brown and Haas, 2012).

3 These authors also link the high degree of euroization in transition economies to the macroeconomic instability in the past which led to high inflation and local currency depreciation in these economies.

A year later in 2011, the Korean government banned banks and other financial institutions from investing in foreign-currency denominated bonds ("Kimchi Bonds") that were used for conversion into local currency by Korean companies who needed foreign currency financing.

Other countries that have taken measures to restrict the growth of foreign currency loans since 2011 include Angola, Belarus and Serbia. Turkey, where households and business had been able to borrow in foreign currency for many years, banned all household borrowing in foreign currency in June, 2009, though the authorities allowed businesses to continue to keep their foreign currency lines of credit open. The Central Bank of the Republic of Turkey (CBRT) did not provide any justification as to why the practice was ended in its decision statement.[4] However, Ozsoz, Rengifo and Kutan (2015) supported the central bank decision to reduce the banking sector's exposure to sudden devaluation periods, due to the terrible social consequences that could befall the Turkish economy from its exposure to foreign currency denominated credit.

Given empirical evidence and the regulatory actions that have followed, it is clear that monetary authorities believe dollarization amplifies risks to the stability of a country's banking system, particularly in the event of sharp fluctuations in the exchange rate. In the following section we will look at one of these countries (Turkey) in more detail to understand the actions its regulators took by banning foreign currency lending to households.

6.4 Case Study: Turkey

Turkey is one of the success stories of the new millennium. The country, which suffered from high chronic inflation rates in the 80s and 90s, experienced a banking crisis and a major devaluation of its currency in 2001. Despite this, Turkey achieved an average growth rate of 4.327% (despite contractions of 5.7% in 2001 and 4.82% in 2009) between 2000 and 2014. Turkish export volumes increased more than threefold between 2000 and 2013 from an index reading 100 in 2000 to 323 in 2013. Foreign direct investment (FDI) flows into the country increased from less than 1 billion US Dollars in 2002 (0.36% of GDP) to over 12.7 billion US dollars (1.6% of GDP) in 2014. (Source: World Bank Databank)

In the meantime, Turkey is also one of the most dollarized economies in the world. As can be observed in Figure 6.2, lending in foreign currencies has long been preferred by Turkish banks and borrowers. Although regulatory agencies banned foreign currency lending to households in the summer of 2009, as of end of 2014, almost 28% of all loans and 48.3% of all liabilities in the banking system were in

4 Article 17 of the Decree 32 titled "Turk Parasini Koruma Kanunu", issued by the Council of Ministers on June 16, 2009.

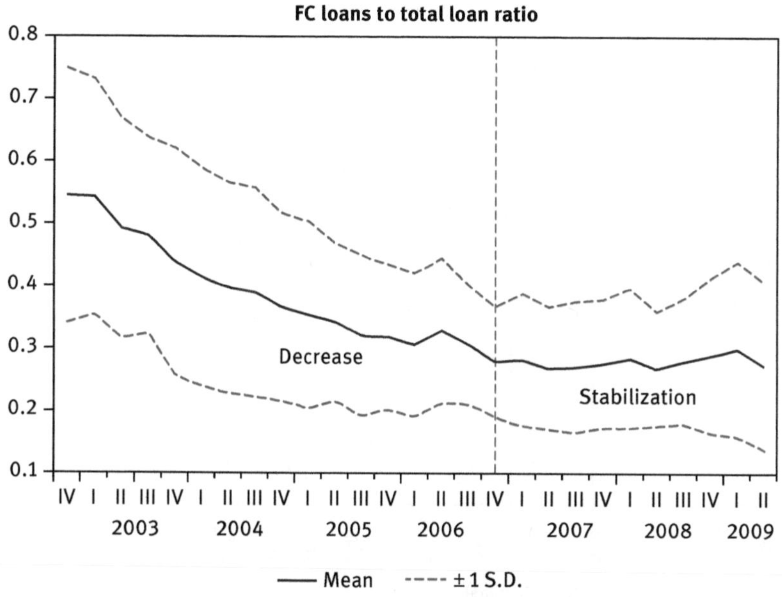

Figure 6.2: Foreign currency loans to total loan portfolio in the Turkish Banking System.
Figure 6.2 shows the average ratio of foreign currency denominated loans to the banks' overall loan portfolio in Turkey with +1/1 standard deviation bounds. The figure covers the fourth quarter of 2002 until the second quarter of 2009.
Source: The Banks Association of Turkey.

foreign currency denominations (Source: The Central Bank of Turkey and The Banks Association of Turkey).

In fact, foreign currency loans have historically constituted a much bigger portion of the banks' loan portfolios in Turkey. As early as in 2002, loans in foreign currency accounted for 54% of the total money lent in Turkey. This figure has gradually dropped to around 27–28% and has been stable at this level since 2009 when the aforementioned regulatory change came into effect. This means roughly one-fourth of all loans in the Turkish banking system are foreign currency denominated.

When we look at the same ratios for the largest (in terms of assets) non-state owned banks,[5] immediately before the regulatory change in Turkey we observe that the picture is not much different. All non-state owned banks by the second quarter of 2009 had foreign currency loans close to 28% of their total loan portfolios. This means both small and large banks[6] adopted foreign currency lending as a favorable hedging

5 Large Non-state owned banks include Akbank, Garanti Bank, Isbank, Yapi ve Kredi Bankasi.
6 Large banks include Akbank, Garanti Bank, Isbank, Ziraat Bank, Vakiflar Bankasi, Halk Bankasi, Yapi ve Kredi Bankasi.

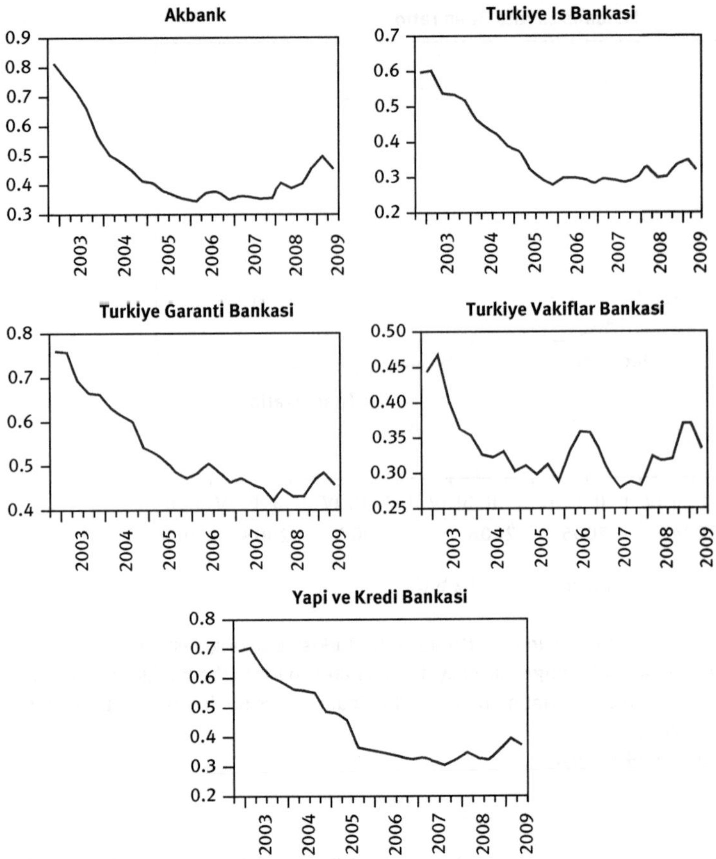

Figure 6.3: Foreign currency loans to total loan portfolio for the largest non-state banks in Turkey. Figure 6.3 shows the ratio of foreign currency denominated loans to overall loan portfolios of the five largest non-state owned banks in our sample. The figure covers 2002-Q4 until 2009-Q2.
Source: The Banks Association of Turkey.

mechanism for their high foreign currency liability portfolio. Such heavy exposure to foreign currency lending must have been a serious cause for concern to regulators (Figure 6.3).

In addition to the high ratio of foreign currency liabilities and loans in the banking system to the overall liabilities and deposits, the Turkish banking system exhibits a rather strong correlation between the two variables (foreign currency denominated deposits and loans). This strong correlation can be observed in Figure 6.4.

Given the strong correlation, Ozsoz, Rengifo and Kutan (2015) examined whether a causal relationship exists between the two variables. By using data from the income

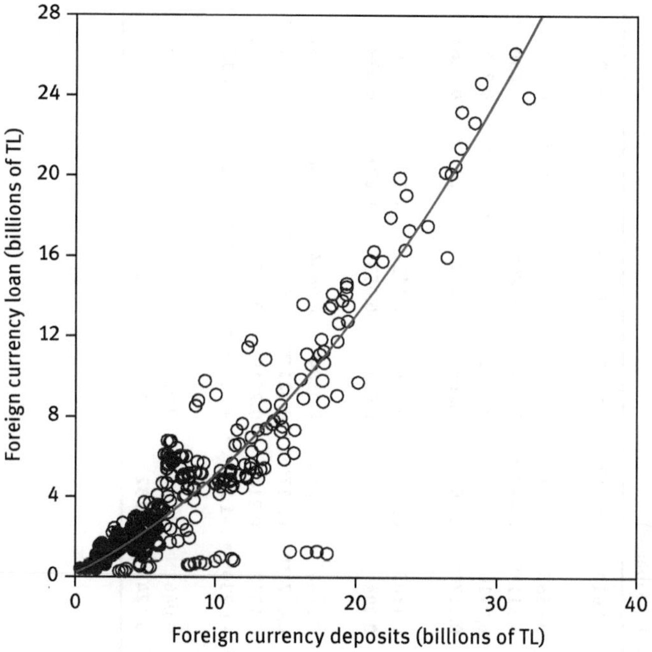

Figure 6.4: Foreign currency loans and deposits in Turkish banking system.
The trend line represents the locus of the fitted values of a 2nd degree polynomial regression of the foreign currency deposits on the foreign currency loans in the banking system of the country for the 2002–2009 period. All figures are in terms of billions of Turkish liras.
Source: Ozsoz, Rengifo and Kutan (2015) and Banks Association of Turkey.

statements and balance sheets of 20 commercial and deposit banks in Turkey for the period covering the last quarter of 2002 and the first half of 2009, the authors estimated the determinants of foreign currency lending by banks in the country. Their estimation takes the following form:

$$\begin{aligned}
& d\left(\frac{loansfc}{loanstotal}\right)_{i,t} = \propto + \beta_1 d\left(\frac{loanstl}{loanstotal}\right)_{i,t} + \beta_2 d\frac{\left(otherassets - cashfc - cashtl\right)}{loanstotal}_{i,t} + \\
& \beta_3 d\left(\frac{depfc}{deptotal}\right)_{i,t} + \beta_4 d\left(\frac{deptl}{deptotal}\right)_{i,t} + \beta_5 d\left(\frac{otherliabilities}{deptotal}\right)_{i,t} + \beta_6 d\left(\frac{equity}{assets}\right)_{i,t} + \beta_7 D_1 \times \\
& d\left(\frac{depfc}{deptotal}\right)_{i,t} + \beta_8 D_2 \times d\left(\frac{depfc}{deptotal}\right)_{i,t} + \beta_9 infvol_t + \beta_{10} dlog\left(liquidityfc\right) + \\
& \beta_{11} dlog\left(liquiditytl\right) + \beta_{12} d\left(gdpgrowth\right)_t + + \mu_i
\end{aligned} \tag{6.2}$$

Table 6.2: Determinants of loan dollarization.

	Dependent variable: First difference of the ratio of foreign currency loans to total loans (d(loansfc/loanstotal))											
Specification	(1)	(2)	(3)	(4)	(5)	(6)	(7)	(8)	(9)	(10)	(11)	(12)
Method	**GMM**	**GMM**	**GMM**	**GMM**	**GMM**	**GMM**	**GMM**	**GMM**	**GMM**	**GMM**	**GMM**	**GMM**
Time period	**2003Q3–2009Q2**	**2003Q3–2009Q2**	**2003Q3–2009Q2**	**2003Q3–2009Q2**	**2003Q3–2009Q2**	**2003Q3–2009Q2**	**2004Q2–2009Q2**	**2004Q2–2009Q2**	**2004Q2–2009Q2**	**2004Q2–2009Q2**	**2004Q2–2009Q2**	**2004Q2–2009Q2**
	Tstatistics (in bold) and Standard errors (below)											
d(loansfc(−1)/loanstotal(−1))	**−0.236*** **	**−0.213*** **	**−0.125** **	**−0.129*** **	**−0.018**	**−0.018**	**−0.010**	**−0.013**	**−0.022**	**−0.026**	**−0.013**	**−0.047**
	0.0111240	0.0249	0.0490	0.0486	0.0163	0.0144	0.0385	0.0538	0.0466	0.0424	0.0569	0.0772
d(depfc/deptotal)		**0.256*** **	**0.127*** **	**0.330*** **	**0.665*** **	**0.663*** **	**0.511*** **	**0.498*** **	**0.473*** **	**0.480*** **	**0.522*** **	**0.630*** **
		0.0097	0.0325	0.1275	0.0613	0.0653	0.0910	0.1365	0.1268	0.1141	0.1604	0.2386
d1*d(depfc/deptotal)			**0.957** **	**1.158** **	**0.207***	**0.198**	**0.257** **	**0.260** **	**0.269** **	**0.251** **	**0.242** **	**0.228***
			0.3910	0.4741	0.1240	0.1311	0.1165	0.1196	0.1281	0.1136	0.1155	0.1408
d2*d(depfc/deptotal)			**0.321**	**−0.083**	**−0.02**	**−0.002**	**0.004**	**0.004**	**0.008**	**0.053**	**0.031**	**0.028**
			0.2389	0.3138	0.0448	0.0646	0.0634	0.0638	0.0584	0.0654	0.0865	0.0961
d(deptl/deptotal)				**0.455*** **	**0.825*** **	**0.860*** **	**0.677*** **	**0.657*** **	**0.621*** **	**0.637*** **	**0.699*** **	**0.775*** **
				0.1615	0.0605	0.0646	0.1367	0.2140	0.2019	0.1816	0.2412	0.2943
d(loanstl/loanstotal)					**−1.140*** **	**−1.141*** **	**−1.230*** **	**−1.231*** **	**−1.217*** **	**−1.144*** **	**−1.177*** **	**−1.125*** **
					0.0179	0.0162	0.0461	0.0475	0.0610	0.0812	0.1157	0.1356
d(equity/assets)						**0.141***	**0.124**	**0.132**	**0.181**	**0.086**	**0.093**	**0.205**

Table 6.2: (continued)

	Dependent variable: First difference of the ratio of foreign currency loans to total loans (d(loansfc/loanstotal))											
Specification	(1)	(2)	(3)	(4)	(5)	(6)	(7)	(8)	(9)	(10)	(11)	(12)
Method	**GMM**	**GMM**	**GMM**	**GMM**	**GMM**	**GMM**	**GMM**	**GMM**	**GMM**	**GMM**	**GMM**	**GMM**
Time period	**2003Q3–2009Q2**	**2003Q3–2009Q2**	**2003Q3–2009Q2**	**2003Q3–2009Q2**	**2003Q3–2009Q2**	**2003Q3–2009Q2**	**2004Q2–2009Q2**	**2004Q2–2009Q2**	**2004Q2–2009Q2**	**2004Q2–2009Q2**	**2004Q2–2009Q2**	**2004Q2–2009Q2**
	Tstatistics (in bold) and Standard errors (below)											
						0.0824	0.1895	0.1961	0.1998	0.2053	0.2072	0.3277
infvol							**0.017**	**0.020**	**0.026**	**0.022**	**0.015**	**−0.024**
							0.0182	0.0310	0.0281	0.0259	0.0307	0.0708
d((otherassets-cashtl-cashfc) / loanstotal)								**0.001**	**0.003**	**0.004**	**0.002**	**0.011**
								0.0081	0.0077	0.0068	0.0093	0.0158
d(otherliabilities/deptotal)									**−0.012**	**−0.012**	**−0.013**	**−0.025**
									0.0199	0.0178	0.0188	0.0279
dlog(liquidityfc)										**−0.002**	**−0.0008**	**−0.0008**
										0.0011	0.0023	0.0027
dlog(liquiditytl)											**0.002**	**0.0007**
											0.0039	0.0039
d(gdpgrowth)												**0.003**
												0.0048

Table 6.2: (continued)

	Dependent variable: First difference of the ratio of foreign currency loans to total loans (d(loansfc/loanstotal))											
Specification	(1)	(2)	(3)	(4)	(5)	(6)	(7)	(8)	(9)	(10)	(11)	(12)
Method	**GMM**	**GMM**	**GMM**	**GMM**	**GMM**	**GMM**	**GMM**	**GMM**	**GMM**	**GMM**	**GMM**	**GMM**
Time period	**2003Q3–2009Q2**	**2003Q3–2009Q2**	**2003Q3–2009Q2**	**2003Q3–2009Q2**	**2003Q3–2009Q2**	**2003Q3–2009Q2**	**2004Q2–2009Q2**	**2004Q2–2009Q2**	**2004Q2–2009Q2**	**2004Q2–2009Q2**	**2004Q2–2009Q2**	**2004Q2–2009Q2**
	Tstatistics (in bold) and Standard errors (below)											
Instruments	d(loansfc/loanstotal), d(deptl/deptotal),d(loanstl/loanstotal),d(equity/assets),infvol,d(otherliabilities/deptotal), dlog(liquidityfc),dlog(cashtl), d(gdpgrowth)											
S.E. of regression	0.07	0.07	0.08	0.08	0.02	0.02	0.02	0.02	0.02	0.02	0.02	0.02
No of banks	20	20	20	20	20	20	20	20	20	20	20	20
J statistic	19.5758	19.06656	15.06224	13.82312	14.16504	11.96152	14.06995	14.13916	13.75596	12.57796	12.43495	11.52393
p value for AR (1)	0.000	0.000	0.000	0.000	0.000	0.000	0.000	0.000	0.000	0.000	0.000	0.000
p value for AR (2)	0.000	0.000	0.000	0.000	0.000	0.000	0.000	0.000	0.000	0.000	0.000	0.000
Observations	454	454	454	454	454	454	397	397	397	397	397	397

Table 6.2 presents the results of GMM estimations on the determinants of foreign currency lending. d represents first differences. ***loanfc/loanstotal*** represents the share of foreign currency loans in respective bank's loan portfolio (adjusted according to the USD-TL exchange rate on October 1, 2002) to the banks' total loan portfolio; ***depfc/deptotal*** is the ratio of foreign currency deposits adjusted according to the USD-TL exchange rate on October 1, 2002 to total deposits; d1 and d2 are dummies to capture the effect of the size of the bank based on its assets; d1 represents banks in the first group (large banks) and d2 represents banks in the second group (medium sized banks); ***liquidityfc*** is the cash holdings of a bank in foreign currency plus foreign currency balances with the central bank; ***liquiditytl*** represents the Turkish lira cash holdings of a bank plus its balance with the central bank in Turkish liras; equity/assets is the ratio of the bank's equity to its assets; ***gdpgrowth*** is the percent change in the seasonally adjusted quarterly GDP growth rate calculated at constant prices; ***deptl/deptotal*** is the ratio of Turkish lira deposits to the total deposits; ***loanstl/loanstotal*** is the ratio of Turkish lira loans to the bank's total loan portfolio; ***(otherassets-cashtl-cashfc)/loanstotal*** is the ratio of bank's assets other than loans and its cash holdings in Turkish liras and other currencies to the bank's loan portfolio and ***infvol*** is the volatility of annual inflation calculated as the three-month standard deviation of annual inflation calculated in a 12 month rolling window.

*Significant at 10%; **significant at 5%; *** significant at 1%.

Source: Ozsoz, Rengifo and Kutan (2015).

Where loanfc/loanstotal represents the share of foreign currency loans in respective bank's loan portfolio (adjusted according to the USD-TL exchange rate on October 1, 2002) to the banks' total loan portfolio; depfc/deptotal is the ratio of foreign currency deposits adjusted according to the USD-TL exchange rate on October 1, 2002 to total deposits; d1 and d2 are dummies to capture the effect of the size of the bank based on its assets; d1 represents banks in the first group (large banks) and d2 represents banks in the second group (medium sized banks); liquidityfc is the cash holdings of a bank in foreign currency plus foreign currency balances with the central bank; liquiditytl represents the Turkish lira cash holdings of a bank plus its balance with the central bank in Turkish liras; equity/assets is the ratio of the bank's equity to its assets; gdpgrowth is the percent change in the seasonally adjusted quarterly GDP growth rate calculated at constant prices; deptl/deptotal is the ratio of Turkish lira deposits to the total deposits; loanstl/loanstotal is the ratio of Turkish lira loans to the bank's total loan portfolio; (otherassets-cashtl-cashfc)/loanstotal is the ratio of bank's assets other than loans and its cash holdings in Turkish liras and other currencies to the bank's loan portfolio and infvol is the volatility of annual inflation calculated as the three-month standard deviation of annual inflation calculated in a 12 month rolling window; "d" represents the difference operator. The results of the authors' estimations are presented in Table 6.2.

Their results suggest that the change in the share of foreign currency deposits to total deposits in Turkey has a significant and positive impact on Turkish banks' lending in foreign currency. The estimated coefficient of this variable is 0.256, which suggests that a 1% change in the share of foreign currency deposits to total deposits raises the ratio of foreign currency loans to total loans ratio by about a quarter percent.

The average magnitude of this variable ranges between 0.12 and 0.66, indicating that a 1% increase in foreign currency deposit ratio could increase the foreign currency loan ratio by as much as 0.66%. This suggests that as banks accept more foreign currency deposits, they tend to lend more in foreign currency. By doing so, Turkish banks are simply transforming their currency risk into default risk, which could arise in case of sudden and large devaluations. In other words, instead of facing a mismatch of assets and liabilities during devaluation, banks potentially face an increasing loan default ratio for their foreign currency denominated loans. This suggests that hedging in the Turkish banking system is almost nonexistent, and a systemic shock due to default risks arising from currency depreciation is a valid and likely possibility. This effect seems to be more pronounced for larger banks as opposed to smaller institutions.

The findings of this research can help us understand the decision taken by the regulatory authorities in Turkey in 2009. An unhedged banking system is vulnerable to sudden exchange rate movements, and we believe this is what the regulators perceived as they introduced their policy change. As seen in earlier emerging market crises (i.e. the East Asian Financial Crisis), mismatches on banks' and financial institutions' balance sheets can have devastating contagious effects during sudden exchange rate movements. Consequently, the decision to end the practice of foreign currency lending in Turkey was an understandable outcome, and is likely to lead to better long-run economic stability, particularly if the country experiences cyclical downturns.

7 Conclusions

Currency substitution or dollarization refers to the use of another country's currency in exchange or in addition to local currency. Dollarization has become a widespread phenomenon in today's global economy.

The dollarization phenomenon can be observed in different forms. Some countries may choose to give up their local currency altogether and adopt another country's currency as legal tender. This type of dollarization is known as "official" or "dejure" dollarization and it is the type of currency substitution currently observed in more than ten countries.

There are many reasons for countries to fully dollarize. In the case of Andorra, Monaco or San Marino it makes perfect sense to adopt the Euro as legal tender. The relatively small size of these economies and each country's economic and political ties with surrounding EU states made using the Euro a necessity. Yet, there are other economies which are not as small in size but also adopted a foreign currency for reasons other than economic or political ties. For instance, Ecuador and El Salvador have chosen this option simply for controlling their runaway inflationary processes.

However, for most economies, dollarization is a de facto process during which local currency slowly loses its roles as a medium of exchange, unit of account and store of value in favor of other "hard" currencies. Known as unofficial or partial dollarization, this type of dollarization usually follows periods of high and chronic inflation.

The link between inflation and dollarization can be understood by realizing that in countries with high inflationary processes, foreign currency provides a shelter from domestic inflation and enables savers to retain the value of their financial assets. The early literature that links inflation to dollarization is known as "currency substitution theory".

In general, interest rate differentials in each currency are predictors of foreign currency holdings. However, recent evidence has shown that dollarization is not only an outcome of inflation. Some dollarized economies (i.e. Argentina, Turkey) were successful in controlling their inflation rates. Yet, despite this success, these economies did not experience a drop in their dollarization ratios. Obviously, this leaves room for new ideas and theories to emerge and explain some of the inefficiencies of orthodox currency substitution theories and the earlier literature that connects the occurrence of dollarization phenomenon to inflation. Noteworthy among these new ideas are the collective memory hypothesis, the minimum variance portfolio view and the institutional theory.

The collective memory hypothesis links the persistence of dollarization to the memories of high and chronic inflation shared by the agents in an economy.

The minimum variance portfolio argues that for a given variability of inflation, an increase in the "variance of the rate of depreciation reduces dollarization by limiting the hedging benefits of dollar assets". This theory further states that stabilization policies aimed at reducing inflation rates may fail to reduce dollarization rates if they also target real rates. This conjecture provides meaningful reasons as to why de-dollarization does not transpire in countries where inflation rates have stabilized. Finally, the institutional view theory links dollarization to the quality of institutions in an economy. The higher the quality of the institutions in a dollarized economy, the more trust economic agents have in the efforts of the monetary authorities to police and keep inflation under control. Economic agents typically only reduce their dollar holdings when they have faith in the institutions that are charged with maintaining economic stability.

There are several benefits and disadvantages of dollarization that differ according to what type of dollarization we examine. For countries fighting high inflation and economic uncertainty, full dollarization provides an easy fix to the inflation problem. In countries that fully adopt another country's currency, both inflation rates and inflation expectations fall over time to the levels experienced in the home country of the adopted currency. This also lowers the country's borrowing costs and enables foreign capital to flow into the economy. Although the monetary authority sacrifices its seigniorage revenue in a fully dollarized economy, this can be regarded as a benefit since it restricts the options available for politicians to finance fiscal deficits. In the long run, the inability to rely on seigniorage revenue fosters budgetary discipline, which is much needed in developing economies.

Full dollarization also enables countries to increase international trade with their main trading partners. Two countries sharing the same currency usually trade more than they would otherwise, and as a result, fully dollarized economies see a growth in their trade with the home economy of the adopted currency. Ecuador, El Salvador and Panama are good examples of this phenomenon.

However, there are costs involved with full dollarization. As the central bank of a fully dollarized economy ceases issuing its currency, it loses its full control of monetary policy. This means in the event of external shocks to the economy, policy makers are limited in their fiscal policy response. For example, one of the main functions of a central bank is to act as the lender of last resort to the banking system in times of economic uncertainty or crisis. In fully dollarized economies, the monetary authority, in addition to loss of its monetary policy, also loses its ability to provide liquidity to the banking system and must rely on its international reserves.

The benefits and disadvantages of full dollarization do not always apply in cases of partial dollarization. In partially dollarized economies, foreign currency denominated deposit accounts enable savings to be channeled into the banking system from "under the mattress".

During inflationary periods, foreign currency accounts also help to prevent capital flight from these economies, as local savers no longer have to take their savings outside their country. By encouraging savings, partial dollarization helps increase the financial depth of an economy. Financial depth refers to the availability of funds, securities and other financial instruments provided by financial intermediaries to final users (individuals, governments and firms). Savings in generate credit for businesses and consumers. Credit enables businesses to expand and consumers to spend, eventually generating economic growth.

However, partial dollarization does not come without its share of drawbacks. Indeed, partial dollarization creates unique challenges for the banking system and puts restrictions on policy makers in these economies.

One of these challenges arises from the fact that the balance sheets of banks in partially dollarized economies contain assets and liabilities in more than one currency. This makes the banks more vulnerable to exchange rate fluctuations as the value of their assets and liabilities change as a result of currency fluctuations.

To rid themselves of the exchange rate risk, banks extend loans in foreign currencies. Having foreign currency assets (loans) in the same amount of their foreign currency liabilities (deposits) would seem like an easy fix for the exchange rate risk the bank faces. If the value of the local currency falls, the balances on foreign currency deposits and loans will rise in the same amount to compensate. However, foreign currency denominated loans may not always be extended to businesses and households that earn their incomes in foreign currency. In the event of devaluation, the bank's balance sheet may show that a bank's assets and liabilities in local currency terms increase at the same amount. However, an increase in the local currency equivalent of a loan balance means borrowers who have earnings indexed to a local currency might be faced with difficulty in repaying loans. Consequently, devaluations might bring about higher default rates for banks on their foreign currency denominated loans. This means that by lending in foreign currency, banks in partially dollarized economies may be only translating currency risk into default risk.

There is empirical evidence that supports the link described above. Recent research (such as Kutan, Ozsoz and Rengifo (2012), De Nicolo, Honohan and Ize (2005)) has shown that banking systems are usually more fragile in dollarized economies where depositors can save and borrow in foreign currencies.

Therefore, in formulating exchange rate and monetary policies, central bankers have to pay close attention to exchange rate fluctuations. Policy makers in dollarized economies usually utilize a variety of targets in formulating their monetary policy. For instance, changes in the reserve requirement for depository institutions include both local currency reserve ratios and also foreign currency deposit ratios.

The Global Financial Crisis of 2008–2009 was a good opportunity for academics and policy makers to see whether the threats posed by dollarization of bank deposits and loans hold in practice.

Research (i.e. Chithu, 2012) showed that real GDP contracted by around 0.84 percentage points more in economies where loan dollarization was 10 percentage points or higher.

The regulatory actions taken by the governments and central banks of some of the most highly dollarized economies also confirm these findings. Following the Global Financial Crisis, regulators in Hungary, Latvia and Poland have tightened eligibility requirements for borrowing in foreign currency and have encouraged banks to use moral suasion to deter retail level foreign currency (FC) borrowing. The authorities in these countries required banks to disclose the exchange rate risks of foreign currency loans to their clients.

In countries like Croatia, Kazakhstan and Romania, stronger provisioning requirements were also imposed on foreign currency lending (Brown and Haas, 2012). Ukraine completely banned FC lending to households in late 2008. In June 2010 the European Central Bank (ECB) stated that national efforts to rein in FX lending in eastern European economies have had little impact and therefore called for coordinated efforts to be taken by EU member states.

Among these efforts, the ECB requested that regulators from banks' home countries which own subsidiaries in Eastern Europe restrict their foreign currency lending (Brown and Haas, 2012).

Turkey, where households and business had been able to borrow in foreign currency for many years, banned all household borrowing in foreign currency in June, 2009, while enabling businesses to continue to keep their foreign currency lines of credit open.

Dollarization is not a process with distinct outcomes that can be prescribed equally to all economies, as the evidence highlighted in this book has shown. Full dollarization helps countries with chronically high inflation rates to reign in price increases, yet leaves central bankers without control of monetary policy. Partial dollarization encourages savings in an economy by providing an alternative method of savings for local depositors. However, the existence of foreign currency deposit accounts on banks' balance sheets creates other risks for the banking system and poses new challenges for central bankers to tackle.

The experiences of partially dollarized economies in the aftermath of the Global Financial Crisis have shown that the dollarization phenomenon is a subject that needs further academic exploration research. We hope our survey and research has provided a path for future dollarization experts to investigate the different dimensions of this phenomenon.

References

Acosta-Ormaechea, S. and Coble, D. 2011. The monetary transmission in dollarized and non dollarized economies: The cases of Chile, New Zealand, Peru and Uruguay. *International Monetary Fund Working Paper Series* WP/11/87.

Alvarez Plata, P. and Garcia-Herrero, A. 2008. To Dollarize or De-dollarize: Consequences for Monetary Policy. *Working Papers 0808*, BBVA Bank, Economic Research Department.

Arteta, Carlos O. 2005. Exchange rate regimes and financial dollarization: Does flexibility reduce bank currency mismatches? *International Finance Discussion Papers* 738, Board of Governors of the Federal Reserve System (U.S.).

Baltagi, B.H. 2008. *Econometrics* (4th ed.). New York: Springer.

Bernanke, B.S., Gertler, M. and Gilchrist, S., 1999. The financial accelerator in a quantitative business cycle framework. *Handbook of Macroeconomics*, 1, pp. 1341–1393.

Berg, A. and Borensztein, E. 2000. The choice of exchange rate regime and monetary target in highly dollarized economies. *IMF Working Paper*, Vol 00/29, pp. 1–32.

Borensztein, E. and Berg, A. 2000. The pros and cons of full dollarization. *IMF Working Paper* No. 00/50, March. Available at: SSRN: http://ssrn.com/abstract=267355 or http://dx.doi.org/10.2139/ssrn.267355 [Accessed September 26, 2014].

Brown, M. and De Haas, R. 2010. Foreign currency lending in emerging Europe: Bank level evidence. *Working Papers* 122, European Bank for Reconstruction and Development, Office of the Chief Economist.

Brown, M. and Haas, R.D. 2012. Foreign currency lending in emerging Europe: Bank-level evidence. *Economic Policy*, 27, pp. 57–98.

Burnside, C., Eichenbaum, M. and Rebelo, S. 2001. Hedging and financial fragility in fixed exchange rate regimes. *European Economic Review*, 45(7), pp. 1151–1193.

Calvo, G. and Vegh Gramont, C. 1992. Currency substitution in developing countries: An introduction. *IMF Working Papers* 92/40.

Carranza, L., Galdon-Sanchez, J. and Gomez-Biscarri, J. 2009. Exchange rate and inflation dynamics in dollarized economies. *Journal of Development Economics*, 89(1), 98–108.

Chang, R. and Velasco, A. 2001. Monetary policy in a dollarized economy where balance sheets matter. *Journal of Development Economics*, 66(2), pp. 445–464.

Chitu, L. September 2012. Was unofficial dollarisation/euroisation an amplifier of the "Great Recession" of 2007–09 in emerging economies? *ECB Working Paper* No. 1473.

Court, E., Ozsoz, E. and Rengifo, E. 2012. The impact of deposit dollarization on financial deepening. *Emerging Markets Finance and Trade*, 48(6), pp. 39–52.

Cuddington, J., Canto, V. and Nickelsburg, G. 1989. Currency substitution: Theory and evidence for Latin America. *Journal of Money, Credit and Banking*, 21(2), p. 267.

Darrat, A., Elkhal, K. and McCallum, B. 2006. Finance and macroeconomic performance. Some evidence for emerging markets. *Emerging Markets Finance and Trade*, 42(3), pp. 5–28.

De Nicoló, G., Honohan, P. and Ize, A. 2005. Dollarization of bank deposits: Causes and consequences. *Journal of Banking & Finance*, 29(7), pp. 1697–1727.

Dehesa, M., Druck, P. and Plekhanov, A. 2007. Relative price stability, creditor rights and financial deepening. *Working Paper* 07/139, International Monetary Fund, Washington, DC.

Delechat, C., Arbelaez, C.H., Muthoora, M.P.S. and Vtyurina, S. 2012. The determinants of banks' liquidity buffers in Central America. *IMF Working Paper* 12/301.

Djankov, S., McLiesh, C., Shleifer, A. 2005. Private credit in 129 countries. National Bureau of Economic Research, *Working Paper* 11078, Cambridge.

Ec.europa.eu. 2016. The euro outside the euro area – European Commission. [online] Available at: http://ec.europa.eu/economy_finance/euro/world/outside_euro_area/index_en.htm [Accessed September 25, 2014].

Edwards, S. and Magendzo, I. 2003. Dollarization and economic performance: What do we really know?. *International Journal of Financial Economics*, 8(4), pp. 351–363.

Eichengreen, B. 2002. Can emerging markets float? Should they inflation target? *Banco Central Do Brasil Working Paper Series* 36.

Eichengreen, B. and Hausmann, R. 1999. Exchange Rates and Financial Fragility. *NBER Working Paper* 7418.

Elkhafif, M. 2003. Exchange rate policy and currency substitution: The xase of Africa's emerging economies. *African Development Review*, 15(1), pp. 1–11.

Feige, E. 2003. Dynamics of currency substitution, asset substitution and de facto dollarisation and euroisation in transition countries. *Comparative Econonomic Studies*, 45(3), pp. 358–383.

Feige, E., Faulend, M., Sonje, V. and Sosic, V. 2001. Currency substitution, unofficial dollarization and estimates of foreign currency held abroad: The case of Croatia, International Finance, EconWPA. Available at: http://EconPapers.repec.org/RePEc:wpa:wuwpif:0106001.

Galindo, A. and Micco, A. 2005. Creditor protection and credit volatility. *Working Paper* 528. Inter-American Development Bank, Washington, DC.

Girton, L. and Roper, D. 1981. Theory and implications of currency substitution. *Journal of Money, Credit and Banking*, pp. 12–30.

Glebocki Keefe, H., Rengifo, E. and Trendafilov, R. 2015. Impact of remittances on frontier markets' exchange rate stability. *Fordham Economics Discussion Paper*, 13(1).

Graff, M., 2003. Financial development and economic growth in corporatist and liberal market economies. *Emerging Markets Finance and Trade*, 39(2), pp. 47–69.

Goldstein, M. 2002. *Managed Floating Plus*, Policy Analyses in International Economics 66. Washington, DC: Institute for International Economics (March).

Hidalgo, J. 2010. Dollarization keeps Ecuador economically stable despite political instability. [Blog] Cato at Liberty. Available at: http://www.cato.org/blog/dollarization-keeps-ecuador-economically-stable-despite-political-instability [Accessed September 26, 2014].

Honig, A. 2009. Dollarization, exchange rate regimes and government quality. *Journal of International Money and Finance*, 28(2), pp. 198–214.

Ize, A. and Yeyati, E.L. 2003. Financial dollarization. *Journal of International Economics*, 59(2), pp. 323–347.

Judson, R. 2012. Crisis and calm: Demand for U.S. currency at home and abroad from the fall of the berlin wall to 2011. International Finance Discussion Papers. *Working Paper* 1058.

Kauffman, D., Kraay, A. and Mastruzzi, M., 2009. Governance matters VIII: Aggregate and individual governance indicators, 1996–2008. *World Bank Policy Research Working Paper*, (4978).

Keefe, H. and Rengifo, E. 2015. Options and central bank currency market intervention: The case of Colombia. *Emerging Markets Review*, 23, pp. 1–25.

King, R. and Levine, R. 1993. Finance and growth: Schumpeter might be right. *The Quarterly Journal of Economics*, 108(3), pp. 717–737.

Kutan, A., Ozsoz, E. and Rengifo, E. 2012. Cross-sectional determinants of bank performance under deposit dollarization in emerging markets. *Emerging Markets Review*, 13(4), pp. 478–492.

Manjani, O. 2012. Estimating the determinants of financial euroization in Albania. *IHEID Working Papers* 07–2015, Economics Section, The Graduate Institute of International Studies.

Manjani, O., 2015. Estimating the determinants of financial Euroization in Albania (No. 07/2015). *Graduate Institute of International and Development Studies Working Paper.*

McKinnon, R.I. 1982. Currency substitution and instability in the world dollar standard. *The American Economic Review*, 320–333.

McKinnon, R. 2000. The East Asian dollar standard, life after death?. *Economic Notes*, 29(1), pp. 31–82.

Medina Cas, S.C., Carrión-Menéndez, A. and Frantischek, F. 2011. The policy interest rate pass-through in central America. *IMF Working Papers*, pp. 1–21.

Menon, J. 2008. Cambodia's persistent dollarization: Causes and policy options. *Asean Economic Bulletin*, 25(2), pp. 228–237.

Miles, M.A., 1978. Currency substitution, flexible exchange rates, and monetary independence. *The American Economic Review*, 68(3), pp. 428–436.

Mongardini, J. and Mueller, J. 1999. Rachet effects in currency substitution: An application to the Kyrgyz Republic. *IMF Working Papers*, 99(102), p. 1.

Morales, J.A. 2003. Dollarization of assets and liabilities: Problem or solution?: The case of Bolivia. *Revista de Análisis*, 6(1), pp. 7–39, Central Bank of Bolivia.

Neanidis, K.C. and Savva, C.S. October 2009. Financial dollarization: Short-run determinants in transition economies. *Journal of Banking & Finance*, 33(10), pp. 1860–1873.

Ortiz, G. 1983. Dollarization in Mexico: Causes and consequences. In P.A. Armella, R. Dornbusch and M. Obstfeld (Eds.) *Financial Policies and the World Capital Market: The Problem of Latin American Countries*, pp. 71–106. Chicago, IL: University of Chicago Press.

Ostry, J., Ghosh, A. and Chamon, M. 2012. Two targets, two instruments: Monetary and exchange rate policies in emerging market economies. *Staff Discussion Notes*, 12(01), p. 1.

Ozsoz, E., Rengifo, E. and Salvatore, D. 2010. Deposit dollarization as an investment signal in transition economies: The cases of Croatia, the Czech Republic, and Slovakia. *Emerging Markets Finance and Trade*, 46(4), pp. 5–22.

Ozsoz, E., Rengifo, E.W. and Kutan, A.M., 2015. Foreign currency lending and banking system stability: new evidence from Turkey. *Central Bank Review*, 15(2), 1–29.

Quispe-Agnoli, M. 2002. Costs and benefits of dollarization. In *Conference on Dollarization and Latin America: Quick Cure or Bad Medicine?* Florida International University, March 4, 2002.

Ramirez-Rojas, C. 1985. Currency substitution in Argentina, Mexico, and Uruguay (Substitution de monnaie en Argentine, au Mexique et en Uruguay) (Sustitucion de moneda en Argentina, Mexico y Uruguay). *Staff Papers – International Monetary Fund*, 32(4), p. 629.

Rose, A. 1999. One money, one market: The effect of common currencies on trade. *NBER, Working Paper* 7432.

Sahay, M.R., Cihak, M., N'Diaye, M.P., Barajas, M.A., Pena, M.D.A., Bi, R., Gao, Y., Kyobe, A., Nguyen, L., Saborowski, C. and Svirydzenka, K. 2015. Rethinking financial deepening: Stability and growth in emerging markets. *International Monetary Fund* No. 15–18.

Savastano, M.M.A. 1996. Dollarization in Latin America: Recent evidence and some policy issues. *International Monetary Fund*.

Snider, M. 2015. Digital currencies and the developing world. Honors Thesis, Fordham University.

Thomas, L.R. 1985. Portfolio theory and currency substitution. *Journal of Money, Credit, and Banking*, 17(3), pp. 347–357.

Végh, C., 1992. Currency substitution in developing countries: An introduction. *IMF Working Paper*, pp. 1–32. Available at SSRN: http://ssrn.com/abstract=884762.

Velickovski, I. and Pugh, G. 2011. Constraints on exchange rate flexibility in transition economies: A meta-regression analysis of exchange rate pass-through. *Applied Economics*, 43(27), pp. 4111–4125.

Yeyati, E.L. 2006. Financial dollarization: Evaluating the consequences. *Economic Policy*, 21(45), pp. 61–118. DOI:10.1111/j.1468-0327.2006.00154.x.

[illegible]

Index

Bei Fragen zur Produktsicherheit wenden Sie sich bitte an:
If you have any questions regarding product safety,
please contact:

Walter de Gruyter GmbH
Genthiner Straße 13
10785 Berlin
productsafety@degruyterbrill.com